The Natural WITCH'S COOKBOOK

100 Magical, Healing Recipes & Herbal Remedies to Nourish Body, Mind & Spirit

LISANNA WALLANCE

In collaboration with
MURIEL TEODORI

Translated by Grace McQuillan

Skyhorse Publishing

Contents

Magic

STILL EXISTS . . . .

In some ways, cooking is a form of magic. A process of transformation. I'm going to show you how to use this knowledge to create healing spells that will serve both your well-being and your desires.

This is not a dusty old book of spells:
it contains witch's secrets that have been adapted for today's tastes. With every recipe you will discover a healing spell.

These recipes are rooted in the magic of the natural world. The secrets to health, joy, and eternal youth are hidden inside plants and unprocessed foods. The nutrients contained in these foods play numerous roles in the human body. Among many other actions, **vitamins A and C** are vital for collagen synthesis and skin repair; **B vitamins** support fertility; **vitamin D** promotes healthy immune system function; and **minerals** like iron and magnesium play key roles in energy production.

But all this is nothing compared to what is possible when we combine certain foods, plants, and herbs: When we do this, we maximize their benefits and let them target specific problems in the body. Whether you're tired, sick, heavyhearted, or simply need a boost for your immune system, fertility, or mood, in this book you'll find just the culinary spell you need. After all, the natural world is the basis of modern medicine. Aspirin comes from the bark of the willow tree, Valium from the valerian root, and antibiotics, of course, come from fungi. You would be right to say that science is very close to magic because they both have a foundation in nature. But don't go thinking that nature is like a scientist or physician. She more closely resembles a witch and a mother. It's just a question of perspective. And perspective can change everything. Life is so complicated when it comes to health and eating that we need a little magic to keep it enjoyable and lighthearted. Loving what you eat and making other people happy are certainly part of cooking, but it can also be seen as a kind of self-care. Imagine this feeling of freedom! What if you could treat your symptoms and those of your loved ones with a little understanding of nature's magic? What if you could make your own immunity and fertility infusions? Or potions that could improve your mood, sleep, and sense of serenity? Imagine delicious recipes that lower cholesterol, aphrodisiac recipes concocted with vegetables, and desserts that are rich in nutrients. Everything is possible!

You only need a little bit of magical knowledge, which draws its power from the elements of earth, air, water, and fire.
Medicinal plants, vegetables, and fruits are full of minerals and vitamins that are hidden in the earth, animals that fly transmit energy and the power of the wind, shellfish and fish that have evolved in the water are filled with good fats and minerals, and land animals are charged with the fire power of the sun: This is why red meat offers essential nutrients. Even the sweet spells, potions, and secrets to eternal youth you'll find in these pages support the body's equilibrium because of the harmony in their ingredients. Everything is connected. You just have to know how to use nature's magic in accordance with your needs.

Magic has been passed down from one culture to another for thousands of years. Midwives, healers, and those who feel connected to the elements and rhythms of earth and the body sense this closeness to nature within them. They are witches. And men can be witches too. I am going to show you how to prepare recipes that no one else will. Unexpected recipes from another realm, another time, and inspired by nature. Recipes that are wildly exotic, unusual but delicious, and most of all, full of magic. And you too, perhaps, will discover your inner witch.

We all have magic hidden within us.

Witches
STILL EXIST . . .

In fact, witches never disappeared . . .
The story of the woman who prepares potions and uses plants and herbs to heal other people has existed since the beginning of time. She is perfectly in tune with nature, the elements, energies, and the rhythm of the seasons. She possesses strong emotions and an intuitive power that accentuates the empathy she feels for others. Her instinctive ability to listen to the body is widely known. She is sometimes called "crazy" or "hysterical," but at least she knows how to use her gifts to maintain control of her own body and life and help people in need.

She takes a keen interest in phytotherapy, naturopathy, nutrition, and alternative therapies. . . . We have already heard about all of these things but don't necessarily associate them with her. She knows how to use food to heal the body, sublimate emotions, and achieve our desires. And cooking is part of this magical art.

Don't you think that in times as complicated as ours, we need witches more than ever?

The Modern WITCH . . .

The witch knows better than anyone how to reestablish the balance between caring for ourselves and enjoying what we eat. She marries the domains of science and reality with those of imagination and natural magic, focusing her efforts on health and a balanced diet.

We are becoming more and more aware of the threat posed to our food sources by pollution and man's impact on nature. And the more we see what is happening the more we are afraid. . . . Food and cosmetic products have too often been corrupted by toxic substances, hormones, and pesticides. But through magic, we can take care of our health while never sacrificing a true passion for food. In a food culture where we oscillate between pleasure and deprivation, and where a focus on health and food can create neuroses, the witch is the person we need to show us how to combine health and well-being.

There must be a way to reconcile the two extremities on the food culture spectrum: the French *gourmandise* and the resolutely American health-conscious approach. The result? Audacious recipes that are out of the ordinary, rich in varied and magical flavors, and created with healthy and healing ingredients.

We must also take care of our earth, because she is part of us. Witches are conscious of this and for this reason prefer homemade, sustainable products. **This is much more than a passion or pastime: it is a lifestyle that everyone should adopt.** The witch is not only someone who cares for humans and respects nature, she is above all a symbol of feminism. Caring for yourself requires loving yourself, listening to your body, and respecting it. Witches represent the liberation of women that accompanies access to knowledge, power, and nature's creations. Today there is a resurgence of feminism and curiosity about magic. It is a political and cultural feminism, a desire for autonomy in our own lives, a concern for ourselves and our future, and concern for the planet. The witch has become a symbol of revolt and protest; **she is emancipation incarnate.** She has existed since the dawn of time and will continue to share her gifts with others. She is, after all, part of nature's spirit.

A History of WITCHES...

We cannot talk about the history of witches without mentioning the representation of women in history. The witch hunts in Europe ended in the 18th century, and the practice of burning women at the stake was motivated by an anti-feminist undercurrent.

These hunts were an attack on women's freedom and their right to practice medicine, which at the time was a career for men. If women demonstrated some interest in science, it was assumed that they were witches. But the real goal of this anti-witch movement was, first and foremost, to extinguish sexual freedom and a woman's right to think for herself. It would seem that people were afraid of their knowledge and power. And even though in later years women were no longer burned at the stake, the events in Salem and the terrible executions that took place in Europe were most likely caused by that same desire to dissuade women from breaking free. Think about the way Shakespeare depicts the evil witches in **Macbeth**, C. S. Lewis's depiction of the witch in **The Chronicles of Narnia**, and the women blinded by sexual jealousy in Arthur Miller's **The Crucible**.

In 1893, an American suffragette named **Matilda Joslyn Gage** offers the first accurate depiction of witch hunts for the first time in **Woman, Church, and State**. She denounced them as an attempt by the church and state to control female sexuality. This text; which paints a faithful portrait of the witch, had a significant impact. Her son-in-law, **Lyman Frank Baum**, author of **The Wizard of Oz**, also created a benevolent witch character, supplanting for the first time the archetype of the evil woman with an ugly face and pointy hat.

The liberation of the witch coincided with women's sexual liberation during the 1960s, but there was still work to be done. There were friendly portrayals of witches like Angela Lansbury's character in **Bedknobs and Broomsticks** and Elizabeth Montgomery's role in the series **Bewitched**, a pretty blonde with blue eyes who embodied the feminine beauty ideals of the time. But there were also, on the contrary, negative depictions in Walt Disney's animated films in which female villains were overcome by jealousy and obsessed with power.

In reality, witches are motivated by a commitment to health and ecology, the lure of knowledge, and the revelation of a better world. Above all, though, theirs is a humanist movement that ultimately concerns women just as much as men (or at the very least their feminine part).

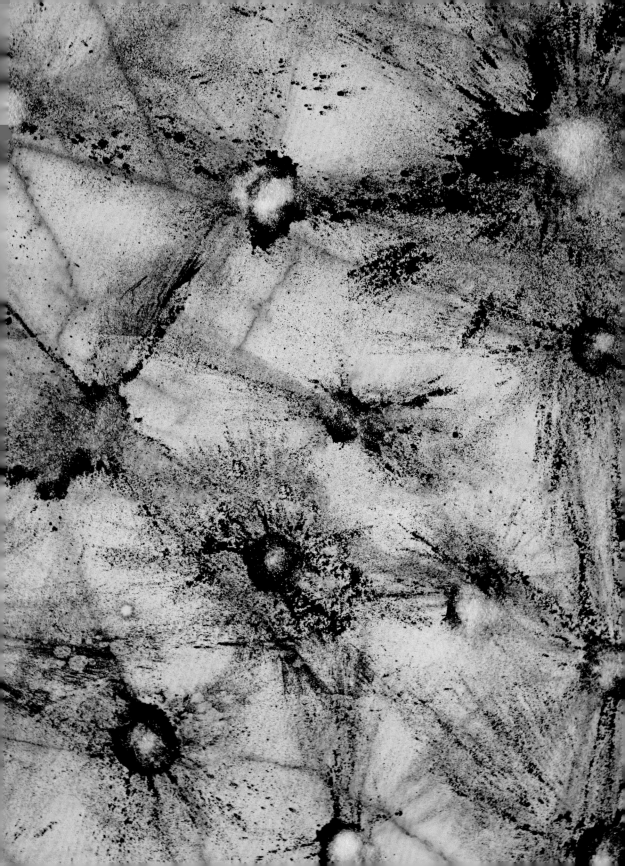

How I Became a WITCH . . .

> Cooking is a form of magic and recipes are like spells. **I realized that I could make people happy, find a way to relieve their health problems, and protect myself from suffering.**

It is possible to become a witch, but very often we are born witches. I didn't dive into the world of cooking and health just for fun; it was out of necessity. One could say that a bad spell had been cast on me at birth: I have Ehlers-Danlos syndrome. This disease makes the collagen in the body fragile and unstable and causes a number of chronic illnesses. Collagen is a protein that is present everywhere in the body. In a way, it is the body's glue: there is not a single organ or structure without it and the whole body is impacted. After college, my symptoms got worse and my life changed. A few of the most serious symptoms include: various pains, digestive, respiratory, and circulatory problems, and autonomic nervous system dysfunction. The peculiar nature of this condition means that its symptoms overlap with other chronic illnesses. I consulted many doctors in the United States (where I was born) and in Paris (where I found love) but many were unsure how to help me when medications failed. I was often referred to someone else, and the cycle would continue.

I decided to turn to myself and to take my body and health into my own hands. I combined my passion for cooking with my fascination with plants and the natural world and used the best of what I found to care for myself. When traditional treatments have reached their limits, healing yourself with food, plants, and herbs is the best possible solution. I spent years experimenting with my diet and trying various natural remedies. I believe that the patient is capable of having the deepest insight into his or her body and pain. I successfully treated my symptoms and regained control of my life thanks to plants and food. My faith in magic has stayed with me ever since. I will never be freed from this disease, because it is chronic, but now I know how to react and treat all of the problems that come with it. Imagination and magic offer a way to find the balance between taking care of your body and delighting your palate. And, more importantly, in the face of physical suffering, they allow us to live in positivity and optimism. Sublimation, after all, is the art of the witch.

My hope is to share this knowledge with you. This book and these magical recipes carry a message: a vow to soothe you, comfort you, and to make you happy. I am sharing *my* spells and secrets with you here so you can, in turn, share this knowledge with others and, most of all, enjoy yourself.

Rebirth Salad (see recipe on p. 27)

Earth
RECIPES

VEGETABLES AND FRUITS
FROM THE EARTH

Of all the elements—earth, water, fire, and air— what comes from the earth remains at the center of a balanced diet. The human body is made up almost entirely of water, and we cannot live without this element, or without air or the warmth of our sun, but the majority of our life force comes from the earth. This element is endowed with almost all of the nutrients, vitamins, minerals, and enzymes that we need to live. And to create vegetables and fruits, the earth calls upon the other elements: water in the form of rain, air with oxygen, and fire with the incredible power of the sun. Even though we can technically live without meat and fish, our body truly does need every nutrient, just in different quantities. Nothing can replace the good fat in fish (water), the amino acids in poultry (air), or the iron and power in meat (fire). But what happens if our diet does not contain any foods that come from the earth? Our body enters a state of complete imbalance that could lead to many health problems. We need the earth's magic more than any other element, and its therapeutic properties are extraordinary: it reinforces our immune, hormonal, and digestive systems, participates in cell regeneration, and protects the body from pollution and toxic chemical products. Plants, after all, are the foundation of modern medicine. By discovering their benefits, learning how to utilize them, and discovering how to potentiate their powers, we can create culinary spells that treat and delight at the same time.

Immunity Mushroom
QUICHE

 SERVES 4-6   30 MINUTES   ⬛ 1 HOUR

Mushrooms bring magic and medicine together. Certain species have incredibly developed immune systems because they have to fight against other invasive mushrooms. They have evolved to become masters of defense. From a biological point of view, they are more closely related to humans than they are to plants. By cooking mushrooms like shiitake and oyster mushrooms, we can benefit from their magical, protective powers. This power comes primarily from their high concentration of vitamin D, an essential nutrient for healthy immune system function. Mushrooms also possess anti-inflammatory, antiviral, and antibacterial properties (think about winter colds and the flu!).

FOR THE ZUCCHINI CRUST

- 2 ZUCCHINI
- 1 TBSP OLIVE OIL

FOR THE MUSHROOM FILLING

- 1 LEEK
- 3½ TBSP (5 CL) OLIVE OIL
- 3 OZ (80 G) BUTTON MUSHROOMS
- 3 OZ (80 G) SHIITAKE MUSHROOMS

- 2 OZ (50 G) OYSTER MUSHROOMS
- 10 FL OZ (30 CL) COCONUT CREAM
- 2 EGGS
- SALT AND PEPPER
- 2 TBSP GOJI BERRIES

THE ZUCCHINI CRUST

▽ Slice the zucchini as thinly as possible. Oil a cake pan (springform is best) with olive oil and arrange the zucchini slices in concentric circles overlapping one another on the base of the pan. Don't forget to put a layer along the edge of the mold to form the side of the crust. Repeat the process to make a second layer.

THE MUSHROOM FILLING

▽ Separate the white part of the leek and mince it (save the green part for Bone Broth, page 159). Heat the olive oil in a pan over high heat and cook the leek until tender, about 10–15 minutes. To achieve a nice caramelization, add a few spoonsful of water to deglaze the pan during cooking and scrape the juices from the bottom of the pan with a wooden spoon.

▽ Preheat the oven to 400°F (200°C).

▽ Set aside a few whole mushrooms and slice the rest. Add the sliced mushrooms to the pan with the leeks and cook for around 10 minutes. Pour in the coconut cream and allow the liquid to reduce for a few minutes.

▽ In a large bowl, beat the eggs with salt and pepper. Add the mushroom filling, mix well, then pour the entire mixture into the zucchini crust. Arrange the whole mushrooms on the top. Bake for 20–25 minutes. Sprinkle with goji berries full of vitamin C, beta-carotene, and zinc, which are essential for good immune health.

▽ Serve the quiche warm. You can also prepare it ahead of time and keep it refrigerated before putting it in the oven.

WITCH'S SECRET

There is a simple spell for increasing the vitamin D content in shiitake mushrooms. Just put them in the sun, gills up, for six hours, and their vitamin D level will increase significantly!

WITCH'S SECRET

Want to cook vegetables of all different sizes so they will be done at the same time? Oven roast vegetables that take longer to cook (like beets, turnips, and carrots) 10–15 minutes before the others. Onions, broccoli, pumpkin, and sweet potatoes cook faster.

Rainbow Roasted
VEGETABLES

 SERVES 4–6 20 MINUTES 30 MINUTES

This culinary enchantment offers earth elements of every color in a single recipe. **Witches know that in the plant world, each color has its own magical property**. Green vegetables are rich in elements that strengthen the heart and reduce inflammation. Red vegetables are charged with beta-carotene that intercepts dangerous free radicals (sun, pollution) and protects the body from cell damage. Yellow and orange vegetables contain a form of beta-carotene that promotes collagen formation, and which are also good for the heart. Purple vegetables are rich in antioxidants that fight cellular aging and protect the heart from blood clot formation (wine is also considered a "purple" food!). Even white vegetables and roots contain antioxidants. These are only a few of the vast benefits of this rainbow of nutrients. We can follow these color codes to focus our diet on specific vitamins and minerals, but we can make vegetables even more magical by serving them together as a rainbow. The result is a dish that covers all of the body's needs: a perfect balance!

FOR THE MARINADE

- **2** GARLIC CLOVES
- **4** TBSP **(6 CL)** OLIVE OIL
- **2¾** TBSP **(4 CL)** BALSAMIC VINEGAR
- **1** TBSP MUSTARD
- **1** TSP HONEY
- SALT AND PEPPER

FOR THE COLORFUL VEGETABLES

GREEN:
- ½ HEAD BROCCOLI
- **10** BRUSSELS SPROUTS

- **2** ZUCCHINI
- ½ BUNCH GREEN ASPARAGUS

RED:
- **2** BELL PEPPERS
- **2** TOMATOES

PURPLE:
- **2–3** COOKED BEETS
- ¼–½ HEAD RED CABBAGE
- **5** BLACK CARROTS
- **2** RED ONIONS

YELLOW/ORANGE:
- **2** SWEET POTATOES
- ½ PUMPKIN
- **5** CARROTS

WHITE:
- **2** WHITE ONIONS

- **3** TURNIPS
- ½ BUNCH WHITE ASPARAGUS
- **4–5** GARLIC CLOVES
- **2** FENNEL BULBS

FOR THE AVOCADO-SHALLOT SAUCE

- **2** SHALLOTS
- **5** BASIL LEAVES
- **1** AVOCADO
- **4½** OZ **(125 G)** YOGURT
- **2** TSP WHITE BALSAMIC VINEGAR OR LEMON JUICE
- SALT AND PEPPER

THE MARINADE

▽ Peel and finely mince the garlic cloves. Whisk together all the marinade ingredients in a bowl.

▽ Peel and chop vegetables of your choosing and cover them with the marinade, making sure everything is coated thoroughly. Spread out all of the vegetables on a baking tray lined with parchment paper and bake for around 30 minutes until they are tender and starting to brown.

THE AVOCADO-SHALLOT SAUCE

▽ Peel and mince the shallots. Remove the basil leaves from the stem and mince finely. Scoop out the avocado flesh. Blend all of the ingredients together until you have a silky sauce.

▽ Serve the vegetables warm from the oven with the avocado sauce on the side.

Revitalization SOUP

 SERVES 4–6  15 MINUTES 30 MINUTES

We've all heard of recipes and foods that are good for the heart, digestion, and cholesterol, but what about foods that are good for the blood? Not as much . . . This is surprising considering that blood is our greatest life force. While all green vegetables are wonderful for our health, certain ones improve blood production (and red blood cell production) in particular. I'm talking about watercress, broccoli, and spinach, which are all high in vitamin K, a blood nutrient, vitamin C, which supports immunity, and antioxidants that regenerate the organs and protect the body. Good circulation and healthy blood (and, as a result, healthy bones) are crucial. When fundamental mechanisms like blood cell production are working well, everything functions better. When you are tired, sick, or under physical and emotional stress, the body needs a little boost, and everything begins with the blood.

- 1 HEAD BROCCOLI
- ½ LARGE SWEET POTATO (OR 2 SMALL ONES)
- 3 ONIONS
- 1 LEEK
- 2–3 HANDFULS OF SPINACH
- 1 BUNCH WATERCRESS
- 3 GARLIC CLOVES, MINCED

- 2 CHICKEN OR VEGETABLE BOUILLON CUBES
- ⅓ OZ (10 G) FRESH GINGER (OR ½ TSP GROUND GINGER)
- ⅛ OZ (5 G) FRESH TURMERIC (OR ½ TSP GROUND TURMERIC)
- SALT AND PEPPER
- 68 FL OZ (2 LITERS) OF WATER

- 2 TBSP WHITE BALSAMIC VINEGAR OR LEMON JUICE
- 1 TBSP VIRGIN COCONUT OIL
- 2 TBSP COCONUT CREAM
- PUMPKIN SEEDS

▽ Chop all of the vegetables into small pieces and add them to a large pot along with the spinach, watercress, minced garlic, bouillon cubes, and crushed ginger and turmeric. Add salt and pepper to taste, then cover with 68 fl oz (2 liters) of water.

▽ Cover the pot and boil the potion for 20–30 minutes until vegetables are tender.

▽ Using an immersion blender, blend the vegetables into a puree. Add the vinegar, coconut oil, and coconut cream, and serve the potion hot with a few pumpkin seeds and a drizzle of oil and coconut cream for decoration.

▽ You can also freeze this soup and save it for a day when you feel the need for revitalization.

WITCH'S SECRET

Always add good fats (olive oil, virgin coconut oil, or nut oils) to vegetables. They need fat in order to be absorbed by the body. To make soups more interesting, I also recommend playing with the acidic, fat, salty, and sweet components in each recipe—wine, olive oil, salt, and honey, for example. It's all about finding a balance between the flavors.

Sunrise
FRUIT

 SERVES 4 10 MINUTES  15–20 MINUTES

Are you looking for a way to get your daily dose of fruits, antioxidants, and fiber early in the morning? Eat a persimmon! This sunrise-colored fruit possesses anti-inflammatory properties and its flavonoids (antioxidants) protect the heart. Oats are a good source of fiber and also support heart health by flushing out the digestive system, balancing cholesterol levels, and supporting arteries. Berries are filled with elements that protect the body from oxidizing stress which causes cell damage and premature aging. I suggest serving this sunrise fruit with a little goat milk yogurt, which is not only easier to digest than yogurt made from cow's milk because of its lower lactose levels but is also richer in enzymes that promote digestion. What's more, goat's milk creates less inflammation in the body than most other dairy products. Starting your morning with the right amount of fiber and antioxidants all in one fruit is the perfect start to a magical day!

- **4** PERSIMMONS
- **3½** OZ **(100** G**)** OATS
- **2** OZ **(50** G**)** FLAX SEEDS
- **2** OZ **(50** G**)** PUMPKIN SEEDS
- **1** HANDFUL OF BERRIES (BLUEBERRIES, BLACK CURRANTS, RASPBERRIES, POMEGRANATE SEEDS)
- **1–2** TSP HONEY
- **⅛** TSP GROUND CLOVES
- GOAT MILK YOGURT

▽ Preheat the oven to 350°F (180°C).

▽ Slice off the top of each persimmon and remove some of the flesh to make room for the filling.

▽ In a small bowl, mix together all of the other ingredients (except the yogurt). Set aside a few berries for decoration at the end. Spoon some of your filling into each persimmon. Put the top of each fruit back on and bake for 15–20 minutes.

▽ Serve these sunrise fruits decorated with berries or a little goat milk yogurt.

Aphrodisiac
BEET TARTARE

SERVES 2   15 MINUTES

Beets were the Viagra of the ancient Romans. According to legend, they would drink beet juice to increase their libido. **Not only are beets filled with powerful antioxidants, they also offer other interesting benefits in terms of . . . physical performance.** The nitric oxide found in beets accelerates blood flow, exactly like cayenne pepper and ginger. It is also rumored that ginger was one of the ingredients in the love potion prepared by Louis XV's mistress (she was probably a little bit of a witch too). The mango (also called the "love fruit") used in the tartar sauce is rich in vitamin E, which helps balance sex hormones. Even the little capers are filled with minerals that stimulate circulation, and apparently these buds were at one time used as aphrodisiacs, too. Oysters can't possibly compete with these aphrodisiac foods! Brought together in a single bewitching dish, these ingredients potentiate their powers and create a vegetarian tartare that lovers will find very stimulating.

- 17½ oz (500 g) COOKED BEETS
- ½ CUCUMBER
- 1 OZ (30 G) CAPERS

FOR THE MANGO LOVE DRESSING

- ½ MANGO
- 1 SHALLOT
- ½ TSP LEMON JUICE

- A FEW CILANTRO OR PARSLEY SPRIGS
- ⅛ OZ (5 G) FRESH GINGER
- PINCH OF CAYENNE PEPPER
- SALT

▽ Finely dice the beets and cucumber and place them in a large bowl. Add the capers and combine..

THE MANGO LOVE DRESSING
▽ Peel the mango and shallot. Dice the mango and mince the shallot. In a bowl, combine the mango, shallot, lemon juice, cilantro leaves (set a few aside for decoration), grated ginger, cayenne pepper, and salt. Use an immersion blender to blend into a puree.

▽ Toss the beet and cucumber cubes with the mango dressing.

Serve the tartare on individual plates and decorate with fresh cilantro or parsley.

WITCH'S SECRET

Do you want to maximize the effects of this aphrodisiac enchantment? Add 1 tsp of maca root powder to the mango dressing before blending it. I guarantee that your lover won't notice the taste of this magic ingredient, but he or she will definitely feel its effects....

Winter Gemstone
SALAD

 SERVES 2   15 MINUTES   2–3 MINUTES

Sweet and juicy citrus fruits are filled with curative properties. Each mouthful of this gemstone salad is a little explosion of flavors and vitamins. A single clementine contains the recommended daily intake of vitamin C. This vitamin is essential for skin regeneration, collagen production, and healthy functioning of the immune system. Grapefruit possesses the same benefits and also has a strong satiating effect thanks to its antioxidants, which boost metabolism. It also has antiviral, antibacterial, and anti-inflammatory properties: a real superfood that can help you avoid winter illnesses! To amplify these benefits, I'm adding a healthy dose of rosemary for its immunostimulant properties and because it goes wonderfully with citrus and balsamic vinegar. Winter is the season for citrus fruit, because nature gives us what we need at just the right moment, and witches can certainly attest to that!

- **4** CLEMENTINES
- **1** GRAPEFRUIT
- **1** POMEGRANATE
- **3½–5** OZ (100–150 G) MACADAMIA NUTS
- A FEW ROSEMARY SPRIGS

FOR THE ROSEMARY DRESSING

- **2** ROSEMARY SPRIGS
- **1** TBSP OLIVE OIL
- **2** TSP BALSAMIC VINEGAR

- **½** TSP HONEY
- SALT AND PEPPER

▽ Peel the clementines and the grapefruit and remove the fine membrane around each segment. Cut the pomegranate in half and remove the seeds. You will need half of the seeds for this recipe; save the rest to use in other recipes like the Creation Honey Pork Roast (p. 111).

▽ Crush the macadamia nuts and dry roast them directly in a pan for a few minutes. Toss frequently until they are toasted on all sides.

THE ROSEMARY DRESSING

▽ Pull off the rosemary leaves from the stem and finely chop them. In a large bowl, combine the ingredients for the dressing and mix well. Add the clementine and grapefruit segments to the bowl and gently toss until each slice is coated with the dressing.

▽ Divide the salad onto individual plates and top each one with the toasted macadamia nuts, fresh rosemary, and a few pomegranate seeds.

▽ You can serve this salad to open a meal and even between courses to refresh the palate.

WITCH'S SECRET

Leftover salad? Don't throw it out! You can transform it into a dressing for another salad. Blend it into a puree and add 1 or 2 tbsp of balsamic vinegar and olive oil depending on your tastes. This dressing will keep in the refrigerator for several days.

Rebirth
SALAD

❧❧❧ 🍽 SERVES 2 ⏱ 10 MINUTES ❧❧❧

With the end of winter and the return of the sun, the earth reveals health benefits hidden in unexpected places, like new plant shoots. These little sprouts offer even more nutrients than adult plants. We always think it's best to eat large quantities of vegetables, but little sprouts give us a concentrated amount of vitamins, enzymes, and minerals. The process of germination increases the levels of protein, folic acid, magnesium, phosphorous, and vitamins C and K. These levels decline as the plant grows. New shoots also have higher quantities of amino acids and are a great option for people with digestive problems because of their significant levels of fiber. One of the best examples is spirulina, the base ingredient for this salad's dressing. This deep blue-green microalga is packed with incredible amounts of antioxidants and vitamins like B12 as well as iron and several other minerals. Who would have thought that a salad made out of microshoots, little green peas, radishes, and sprouted seeds could offer about the same benefits as a double serving of vegetables?

FOR THE SPIRULINA DRESSING

- ZEST AND JUICE OF ½ LEMON
- ½ GARLIC CLOVE
- ⅛ TSP SPIRULINA POWDER
- 1 TBSP OLIVE OIL
- ¼ TSP MUSTARD
- SALT AND PEPPER

FOR THE REBIRTH SALAD

- 17½ OZ (500 G) FRESH PEAS
- 9 OZ (250 G) RADISHES, SLICED
- 3½ OZ (100 G) MICROSHOOTS FROM RADISH, ALFALFA BROCCOLI OR PEA PLANTS
- ¾ OZ (20 G) PUMPKIN SEEDS
- FRESH MINT

THE SPIRULINA DRESSING

▽ Zest the lemon, peel and finely mince the garlic. In a large bowl, whisk together all of the ingredients for the dressing with a pinch of salt and pepper.

THE SALAD

▽ Add the peas, sliced radishes, and washed and dried sprouts to the bowl with the dressing. Mix well.

▽ Serve the salad with a sprinkling of pumpkin seeds and chopped mint. You can also keep this salad in the refrigerator and serve it the next day!

WITCH'S SECRET

To maximize the benefits of raw seeds like pumpkin seeds as well as walnuts, almonds, and even lentils, just soak them in a bowl of water overnight to activate their hidden nutrients and make them easier to digest.

Vegetable Purees in
HEALING COLORS

 SERVES 4–6   🕐 15 MINUTES   ⬛ 20 MINUTES

Even though it's important to always chew your food, culinary magic offers us a delicious shortcut in the form of purées! We can save energy that can then be directed elsewhere: toward our immune system, cell renewal, or the process of digestion itself, for example. Feeling tired? A little down? Or is your digestion seeming a little sluggish? Eat vegetables in the form of a puree. When you make a puree, you're breaking down fiber and proteins before they enter the stomach, and this means the pancreas doesn't need to produce as many enzymes to break down food so the body can absorb the vitamins and minerals. And nutrition aside, I think that purées also increase the vegetables' flavor . . .

FOR THE GREEN PUREE

- 1 HEAD BROCCOLI
- ½ CELERY ROOT
- ⅛ OZ (5 G) FRESH GINGER
- ¼ TSP SPIRULINA
- 2 TSP OLIVE OIL
- SALT AND PEPPER

FOR THE ORANGE PUREE

- 1 SWEET POTATO
- ½ PUMPKIN
- 3 STAR ANISE PODS
- 6 CARDAMOM PODS
- 2 TSP COCONUT OIL
- SALT AND PEPPER

FOR THE PURPLE PUREE

- ½ HEAD RED CABBAGE
- 3 RAW BEETS
- ¼ TSP GROUND CLOVES
- 1 TSP BALSAMIC VINEGAR
- 2 TSP OLIVE OIL
- SALT AND PEPPER

For this recipe you will need three pots.

▽ First, prepare the vegetables: Remove the florets from the head of broccoli, peel and slice the celery root. Peel the sweet potato and slice it. Do the same with the pumpkin. Chop the red cabbage. Peel and slice the beets. Cut all of the vegetables into pieces roughly the same size. Peel and grate the ginger. Crush the cardamom pods to release the aromatic seeds.

▽ Place the ingredients for each puree (except the oils) in a pot filled with water. Add salt and pepper.

Bring to a boil and cook until you can easily pierce the vegetables with a knife, about 20 minutes.

▽ Empty the remaining water from each pot (and remove the cardamom seeds from the orange puree).

▽ Blend the vegetables into a puree and finish by adding the respective oils indicated in the recipe. Serve all 3 purées on each plate or in separate bowls.

WITCH'S SECRET

Make sure you don't swallow the purées like a drink. It's important to chew and give the food time to mix with your saliva—this is an essential part of digestion. Saliva may do less work than stomach acid and digestive enzymes, but "chewing" these purées even a little bit will guarantee better digestion.

Superpower SALAD

 SERVES 4   15 MINUTES   10 MINUTES

Superfoods are foods that are particularly rich in nutrients and health benefits. But how can you recognize them? Even if you don't have a witch's knowledge, just take a look at recent food trends. First there was quinoa, a grain-like seed that unlike many others is a complete source of protein, meaning that it contains all of the essential amino acids. Then there was kale, which is filled with antioxidants and possesses detoxifying properties similar to spinach, and then avocados became all the rage because of their healthy omega-3 fatty acids. But there are so many other superfoods. The beet, for instance, is one of our greatest detox allies for liver health. And why not maximize these superpowers by using several superfoods in one spell?

- **4** KALE LEAVES
- **4½** OZ **(125 G)** SPINACH
- **4** COOKED BEETS
- **1** SWEET POTATO
- **3–5** QUAIL EGGS
- **1** HANDFUL OF BERRIES (RASPBERRIES, BLUEBERRIES, POMEGRANATE SEEDS)
- **1** AVOCADO, DICED

FOR THE HERB DRESSING

- FRESH HERBS (BASIL, PARSLEY, CORIANDER)
- **½** GARLIC CLOVE
- **1** TBSP OLIVE OIL
- JUICE OF **½** LEMON
- **½** TSP MUSTARD
- **¼** TSP HONEY
- SALT AND PEPPER

▽ Preheat the oven to 350°F (180°C).

▽ Chop the kale into small pieces, keeping only the leaves, not the tough stem. Spread out the leaves on a baking tray lined with parchment paper. Bake for 5–7 minutes until crispy.

THE HERB DRESSING

▽ Finely chop the fresh herbs. Peel and mince the garlic. In a large bowl, combine all of the ingredients for the herb dressing and mix well. Next add the spinach leaves and chopped beets and coat them with dressing.

▽ Peel, slice, and cook the sweet potato in boiling water for 10 minutes with the quail eggs. Drain the sweet potato and add it to the salad, warm. Carefully peel the quail eggs and cut them in half.

▽ Incorporate the berries, diced avocado, and halved quail eggs. Gently mix the salad and serve immediately with crispy kale on top for decoration. (Add the kale at the last minute to make sure it stays crispy.)

Balsamic Carrots
FOR A RADIANT COMPLEXION

 SERVES 4    10 MINUTES   25 MINUTES

There's a reason why foods the color of the sun promote radiant skin. This orange or red pigment comes from the presence of beta-carotene, an antioxidant converted into vitamin A by the body. This vitamin is critical for skin and cell renewal as well as collagen production. This healthy skin spell involves caramelizing the carrots in balsamic vinegar until they are grilled on the outside and soft on the inside. And for a gourmet touch, you'll find a sauce made from squash cooked in coconut cream that's filled with fats that nourish the skin and help with vitamin A absorption. If you feel like practicing a little magic with this ingredient in a potion for eternal youth, I'd suggest the Sun Oil on page 194.

FOR THE SQUASH SAUCE

- ½ JAPANESE (OR BUTTERNUT) SQUASH
- OLIVE OIL
- 6¾ FL OZ (20 CL) COCONUT CREAM
- 1 TSP CURRY POWDER
- ½ TSP GROUND CUMIN

- SEEDS FROM 4 CARDAMOM PODS
- SALT

FOR THE CARROTS

- 2 TBSP OLIVE OIL
- 1 BUNCH CARROTS, PEELED

- 3½ TBSP (5 CL) BALSAMIC VINEGAR
- SALT AND PEPPER

THE SQUASH SAUCE

▽ Peel the squash and cook it in a pot of boiling water with a little bit of oil until it becomes tender. Drain the water. Use an immersion blender to blend the squash into a puree. Add the coconut cream, spices, and salt, and let this mixture reduce over low heat for 5 minutes until the sauce is thick and creamy.

THE CARROTS

▽ Heat the oil in a large pan over high heat. Add the peeled carrots and let them cook for 10 minutes, stirring frequently. Deglaze the pan with the balsamic vinegar. When the vinegar has reduced somewhat, add salt and pepper then cover the pan and let cook for 10 minutes until the carrots are very tender.

▽ Serve the carrots with the warm squash sauce.

WITCH'S SECRET

If you don't have time to stand next to a pan, you can also make this recipe in the oven. Just cover the carrots with the olive oil and balsamic vinegar and bake for 15–20 minutes at 400°F (200°C).

WITCH'S SECRET

You can use this same dough for sweet tarts! I suggest one made with dates and chocolate. For the filling: Make a puree using 1 avocado, 14 oz (400 g) of melted chocolate, and 1 oz (30 g) of honey. Pour this mousse into the blind-baked pastry crust and refrigerate for 2 hours before serving.

Rebirth Autumn
ROOT TART

 SERVES 6 15 MINUTES ☐ 45 MINUTES

Spring is the season of rebirth. The earth thaws and gives us new shoots and several vegetables and fruits. **But there is a second time of creation during the year that may bring even more benefits.** Autumn produces fruits, nuts, and root vegetables that are hidden in the earth and filled with minerals, vitamins, and antioxidants that improve immune system function. This is the earth's way of giving us everything we need to survive the winter. Like nuts and fruits, the roots—still saturated with summer sun—are plants' energetic center and life force. They are also incredibly rich in protective nutrients. This tart embodies the earth's magic and pays homage to the healing vegetables of autumn.

FOR THE FRUIT AND NUT CRUST

- **3½ OZ (100 G)** PITTED DATES
- **3½ OZ (100 G)** GROUND ALMONDS
- **3½ OZ (100 G)** FLOUR **+** EXTRA FOR THE WORK SURFACE
- **2 TBSP** OLIVE OIL
- **1** EGG
- SALT AND PEPPER

FOR THE ROOT FILLING

- **2** RED ONIONS, DIVIDED
- **6** SHALLOTS, DIVIDED
- **2 TSP** OLIVE OIL
- SALT AND PEPPER
- **13½ FL OZ (40 CL)** CRÈME FRAÎCHE (OR SOUR CREAM OR COCONUT CREAM)
- **1** CARROT
- **1** COOKED BEET
- THYME AND ROSEMARY
- SALT AND PEPPER

▽ Preheat the oven to 350°F (180°C).

THE FRUIT AND NUT CRUST
▽ Blend all of the ingredients for the crust together with a food processor or an immersion blender until they are thoroughly combined and form a ball. On a floured work surface, roll out the dough into a disc slightly wider than your springform cake pan. Line the cake pan with the dough and poke holes in the base with a fork to prevent the crust from puffing up during baking. Bake for 15 minutes until golden brown and crisp. Monitor the baking carefully, because the natural sugars in the dates cause the crust to burn more easily. If the sides of the crust start to bake too quickly compared to the base, you can line the edges with aluminum foil.

THE ROOT FILLING
▽ Dice 1 onion and 3 shallots (save the rest for decoration) and panfry them with the oil, salt, and pepper for around 10 minutes until caramelized. Add a splash of water when the onions begin to stick to the pan to deglaze and bring out natural sugars. Add the crème fraîche and reduce until the mixture has the consistency of a thick sauce.

▽ Peel the second onion and the remaining shallots and cut them in half. Peel the carrot and slice it into half-inch rounds. Boil these root vegetables for 10 minutes. Remove them from the water and let dry on a paper towel. Slice the beet in half.

▽ Pour the onion cream filling into the pastry crust, then arrange the boiled roots and beet halves on top, drizzle them with olive oil, and bake the tart for around 30 minutes.

▽ Just before serving, garnish the tart with fresh herbs like thyme and rosemary.

Detox
RISOTTO

 SERVES 4   10 MINUTES   35 MINUTES

When we think of risotto we usually think of a rich dish, and even though nothing can replace a real risotto Milanese, we can make a healthier version that is just as delicious. In reality, rice is poor in nutrients compared to other grains, and this recipe for a quinoa and vegetable detox risotto contains a tremendous amount of minerals and vitamins. Quinoa is full of complex carbohydrates, contains more protein than rice, and its insoluble fiber—meaning fiber that can't be digested—helps cleanse the digestive system of toxins, cholesterol, excess hormones, and inflammation markers. Beets are also anti-inflammatory and very rich in antioxidants thanks to their red color. (Need a rule of thumb for your health that's easy to remember? Eat dark-colored produce!) And like beets, radishes are particularly helpful for supporting the liver's natural detox mechanisms. For better health, choose this version instead of a gourmet risotto with Parmesan . . . most of the time.

- **2** TBSP OLIVE OIL, DIVIDED
- **3** SHALLOTS, MINCED
- **9** OZ **(250** G**)** QUINOA
- **6¾** FL OZ **(20** CL**)** RED WINE
- **5** RAW BEETS (OR **17-½** OZ **(500** G**)** COOKED BEETS**)**

- **7–10½** OZ **(200–300** G**)** BRUSSELS SPROUTS
- **34** FL OZ **(1** LITER**)** OF BONE BROTH (P. **159)** OR WATER WITH **1** BOUILLON CUBE
- **½** BUNCH RADISHES

- **3½** TBSP **(5** CL**)** BALSAMIC VINEGAR
- SALT AND PEPPER

▽ Heat 1 spoonful of olive oil in a large pan over high heat. Add the minced shallots and sauté for a few minutes. Next add the quinoa and toast for 1–2 minutes until you smell a nutty aroma. Pour in the wine and mix until it has absorbed completely.

▽ Peel the beets and slice them in quarters. Remove the small stems and outermost leaves from the brussels sprouts and cut them in half. Place the beets and brussels sprouts in another pan with the rest of the oil. Sauté them for a few minutes and transfer to the pan with the quinoa.

▽ Pour over 1 ladleful of broth and stir it into the quinoa until the liquid is completely absorbed.

Repeat this process with the rest of the broth until the quinoa is cooked (the grains will swell and start to "sprout").

▽ Wash the radishes, then add them to the risotto with the balsamic vinegar and a little salt and pepper. Let these detox ingredients infuse for 10 more minutes over low heat, stirring often.

▽ If the risotto has become too dry, you can add a little more broth. Serve it hot. If you want to reheat it in a pan, add a few spoonsful of water or broth to rehydrate it.

WITCH'S SECRET

For any risotto, whether you make it with rice, quinoa, or semolina, there a few "secrets" you should know: cook over low heat, use cold broth and good wine, and when the risotto is ready, turn off the heat and stir in a slice of butter or a drizzle of oil to make it even more delicious.

Fertility Stuffed
SQUASH

 SERVES 4–6 20 MINUTES 1 HOUR 20 MINUTES

With a little culinary witchcraft, we can maximize the benefits of nutrients that nature offers. **Why not cook quinoa inside a whole vegetable the way we cook stuffing inside a turkey? And if wine enhances the flavor of meat, couldn't it do the same for vegetables?** This spell offers undeniable gastronomic pleasure but also supports fertility and reproductive processes. Quinoa is filled with minerals and B vitamins, in particular folic acid (vitamin B9), which is essential during pregnancy. The fiber it contains balances excess hormones in the digestive system and body and its high quantities of zinc promote ovulation. Like quinoa, squash is rich in fiber, B vitamins, and also in vitamin E, vitamin C, and vitamin A (beta-carotene), antioxidants that balance the reproductive system.

- **1** BUTTERNUT SQUASH
- **2** TBSP OLIVE OIL
- **2** RED ONIONS, MINCED
- **3½** OZ **(100 G)** MUSHROOMS, SLICED
- **3½** OZ **(100 G)** RAW QUINOA
- **7** TBSP **(10 CL)** RED WINE
- **2** TBSP BALSAMIC VINEGAR
- SALT AND PEPPER

▽ Preheat the oven to 350°F (180°C).

▽ Cut the squash in half, remove the seeds, and place the squash skin-side up on a greased baking tray. Bake for 30 minutes.

▽ Heat 1 tbsp of olive oil in a pan. Add the minced onions and sliced mushrooms and sauté until tender and caramelized. Next incorporate the quinoa, wine, balsamic vinegar, salt, and pepper. Continue cooking until the liquid is absorbed.

▽ Cover the quinoa with an inch of water. Cover the pan and cook for 15 minutes until the little quinoa grains have almost doubled in size and are starting to "sprout."

▽ Remove the squash from the oven and scoop out some of the flesh with a spoon to make a larger cavity so you can better fill both halves. Fill one of the halves with the quinoa stuffing and cover with the other half. Put the squash back in the oven and cook for 30 minutes. Slice it before serving!

WITCH'S SECRET

To make quinoa even lighter and give it a deeper nutty flavor, I suggest toasting it in a pan with a spoonful of oil for a few minutes before boiling it. Stir often to keep the seeds from burning.

Antioxidant
QUICHE

  SERVES 4–6  30 MINUTES 1 HOUR–1 HOUR 15 MINUTES

Berries aren't the only source of antioxidants. Certain vegetables like artichokes, tomatoes, and sweet potatoes are other rich sources. But what is oxidation? It's a process that harms the body as a cellular level and is brought on by illness, stress, aging, pollution, and exposure to harmful chemical products. This is why it's important to include enough antioxidants in your diet to fight against this inflammation-causing damage. This protection spell is presented as a crustless quiche made from several layers of vegetables that all contain powerful antioxidants. And, of course, there's grilled cheese on top (goat and feta work equally well) for an extra dose of probiotics and, more important, pleasure!

- 2 SWEET POTATOES
- 1 ZUCCHINI
- 2 LARGE TOMATOES
- OLIVE OIL
- 10 OZ (280 G) CANNED ARTICHOKE HEARTS (KEEP THE LIQUID FOR THE FETA CREAM)
- 7 OZ (200 G) GOAT CHEESE
- 10½ OZ (300 G) CHERRY TOMATOES

FOR THE FETA CREAM

- 7 OZ (200 G) FETA
- 4 TBSP (6 CL) JUICE FROM CANNED ARTICHOKES
- 4 EGGS

- A FEW BASIL AND THYME LEAVES, CHOPPED
- SALT AND PEPPER
- 4 OZ (120 G) FLOUR (OR GLUTEN-FREE FLOUR)

▽ Preheat the oven to 400°F (200°C).

▽ Prepare the vegetables: Peel the sweet potatoes. Slice them very thinly and do the same with the zucchini and tomatoes.

THE FETA CREAM
▽ Melt the feta in the microwave. To the melted cheese, add the artichoke liquid, eggs, chopped fresh herbs, salt, and pepper. Then incorporate the flour and mix well.

THE TART
▽ Grease a springform cake pan with olive oil. Cover the bottom with a layer of sweet potato, overlapping the slices. Cover with a layer of feta cream. Add a layer of zucchini and another layer of cream, followed by the tomatoes and a layer of cream. For the last layer, add the artichoke hearts and slices of goat cheese. Slice the cherry tomatoes in half and place them on top of the cheese.

▽ Bake the quiche for 1 hour–1 hour 15 minutes.

WITCH'S SECRET
Would you like to increase the health benefits of your tomatoes? Just dry them in the oven at 250°F (120°C) for 3 hours. This process dramatically increases their levels of lycopene (a very powerful antioxidant that is present in large quantities in tomatoes).

Vegetables for
DIGESTIVE FORTIFICATION

 SERVES 4  10 MINUTES 🔲 40 MINUTES

Spells in the form of recipes always pass through the digestive system because this is the system responsible for properly transmitting healing nutrients to the other systems and organs. To take full advantage of this alimentary magic, we need a digestive system that functions well, but this system can be fairly fragile and can easily be thrown off-balance. Our intestinal microbiota is made up of billions of bacteria concentrated in the colon. This microbiota is determined not only by our genes but also by our dietary habits. Certain foods support intestinal balance and can help restore and fortify digestive function. I'm talking about foods rich in insoluble fiber, like broccoli, red cabbage, and fennel, that help balance and clean out the colon. Vinegar, thanks to fermentation, is filled with natural probiotics that feed the microbiota. Other foods reduce acid in the stomach, like ginger, fennel, and flaxseed. For many, the secret to digestive comfort is making room on your plate every day for antioxidants, a dose of fermented foods, and vegetables and fruits that are rich in fiber.

- ½ RED CABBAGE
- 2 FENNEL BULBS
- 3 APPLES
- 1 HEAD BROCCOLI

- 1 TBSP OLIVE OIL
- 2 TBSP BALSAMIC VINEGAR
- ⅛ OZ (5 G) FRESH GINGER
- SALT AND PEPPER

- JUICE OF 1 LEMON
- 1 TSP FLAX SEEDS

▽ Chop the cabbage, fennel, and apples into small pieces and remove the broccoli florets.

▽ Heat the oil in a pan over high heat. Add the cabbage and sauté for 20 minutes or until tender and caramelized. Pour in the balsamic vinegar and allow the liquid to absorb.

▽ Next add the fennel, broccoli, and grated ginger. Let the vegetables cook until they are tender and caramelized, around 20 minutes. Add salt, pepper, and lemon juice, and let them infuse for a few additional minutes over low heat.

▽ Remove from heat and add the diced apples. Serve the vegetables sprinkled with flax seeds.

▽ To reheat the vegetables the next day, put them in a pan and add a splash of balsamic vinegar to reenergize them.

WITCH'S SECRET

My secret for making vegetables even more delicious? Incorporating a mixture of fat and acidity into my soups and sautéed dishes. I suggest 1 tbsp of virgin olive or coconut oil and red wine, lemon juice, or balsamic vinegar. The two elements combined create a balance of tastes and bring out the complex flavors in the vegetables.

WITCH'S SECRET

When cooking, always add fresh herbs like basil at the end, otherwise they will burn, and you will lose both the flavor and the healing properties.

Green PIZZA

 SERVES 4  20 MINUTES 1 HOUR 15 MINUTES

Ever since childhood, the reminder to "eat your vegetables" has had the power to make us grimace at times . . . **This is a shame, because green vegetables are full of vitamin K (which supports heart health and blood flow), vitamin C (which protects the immune system and the skin), and powerful antioxidants.** The solution, therefore, is to turn to the witch's magic of sublimation. How can we make these vegetables more joyful? By turning them into a pizza! The dough for this green pizza is made with cauliflower, broccoli, and spirulina, and I assure you it is full of flavor. Best of all, thanks to the green magic in the rest of the ingredients, you'll feel energized and light with your pizza cravings satisfied.

FOR THE GREEN DOUGH

- ½ HEAD BROCCOLI
- 1 CAULIFLOWER
- 2½ OZ (70 G) GOAT CHEESE, MELTED
- 1 EGG
- ½ TSP SPIRULINA POWDER
- 1–2 BASIL SPRIGS, MINCED
- SALT AND PEPPER

FOR THE TOMATO SAUCE

- 1 ONION
- OLIVE OIL
- 7 OZ (200 G) TOMATO PUREE
- 8½ FL OZ (25 CL) RED WINE
- FRESH BASIL, CHOPPED
- SALT AND PEPPER

FOR THE TOPPING

- A VARIETY OF GREEN VEGETABLES: ZUCCHINI, BROCCOLI, SPINACH, ASPARAGUS
- OLIVE OIL
- SALT AND PEPPER
- GRATED EMMENTALER OR PARMESAN CHEESE (OPTIONAL)

▽ Preheat the oven to 400°F (200°C).

THE GREEN DOUGH

▽ Separate the broccoli and cauliflower florets and boil them in a pot until you can easily pierce them with the tip of a knife. Drain them and blend into a puree.

▽ Lay out a muslin or dishcloth on the counter, pour the puree into the center and wrap the cloth around it, twisting at the top to extract as much liquid as possible so your crust will be nice and crispy.

▽ In a large bowl, mix the dried dough with the melted goat cheese (microwave the cheese for 20–30 seconds to soften), the egg, spirulina, minced basil, salt, and pepper.

▽ Transfer the dough onto a baking tray that is either greased or lined with parchment paper and use a large spoon to flatten the dough into a disc just under half an inch thick.

▽ Bake the dough for 30 minutes until it is dry and a little brown. Turn it over and bake the other side for 10–15 minutes.

THE TOMATO SAUCE

▽ Chop the onion and sauté in a pan with some oil until tender and translucent. Then add the tomato puree, wine, chopped basil, salt, and pepper and continue cooking over medium heat for 5 minutes.

THE TOPPING

▽ Thinly slice the vegetables. Cover the pizza dough with the tomato sauce and then top with sliced vegetables. Finish with a drizzle of olive oil and some salt and pepper. You can also add a layer of grated Emmentaler or Parmesan on top.

▽ Bake the pizza for 20 minutes.

Restorative Vegetable
CURRY

 SERVES 4   10 MINUTES   30 MINUTES

Everyone has times when they feel off-balance, tired, and weak for no reason. Even when we don't know the true cause of these moments of physical weakness, there are vegetables that can help the body to revive. Brussels sprouts, cauliflower, bok choy, and broccoli all promote healthy immune system function by protecting the body from free radicals (thanks to their high vitamin K and vitamin C content). They are filled with restorative antioxidants, fight inflammation, and help cleanse and balance the digestive system with their insoluble fiber. The coconut and spices in this recipe also protect against inflammation and support digestion. To enhance your culinary spells, always try adding healing herbs and spices.

- **14 OZ (400 G)** BROCCOLI
- **14 OZ (400 G)** CAULIFLOWER
- **7 OZ (200 G)** BRUSSELS SPROUTS
- **2** ONIONS
- **2** BUNCHES BOK CHOY OR ½ HEAD CABBAGE

- **1** TBSP VIRGIN COCONUT OIL OR NEUTRAL OIL
- **2** GARLIC CLOVES, MINCED
- ½ RED CHILE PEPPER, CHOPPED
- **½ OZ (15 G)** FRESH GINGER
- **17–20** FL OZ **(50–60 CL)** COCONUT CREAM

- ½ TSP CURRY POWDER
- ½ TSP GROUND CUMIN
- SEEDS FROM **4** CARDAMOM PODS
- **1** TSP SOY SAUCE
- RICE OR LENTILS
- SESAME SEEDS

▽ Divide the broccoli and cauliflower into small florets. Remove the small stems and outermost leaves from the brussels sprouts and cut them in half. Chop the onions and bok choy.

▽ Heat the oil in a large pan over high heat and add all of the vegetables. Cook for a few minutes until they are roasted. Lower the heat and add the minced garlic and chopped red chile pepper, grated ginger, half the coconut cream, and the spices and cook for 10–15 minutes. Incorporate the rest of the coconut cream and the soy sauce and stir well.

▽ Serve the curry with rice or lentils and sprinkle with sesame seeds.

WITCH'S SECRET

You can amplify this spell with the magic of air or fire by adding chicken or beef. Cut the meat into pieces and sear them in a separate pan. Add the meat to the vegetable curry a few minutes before serving.

WITCH'S SECRET

If you don't have time to prepare the raspberries yourself, buy a premade coulis and cook it with balsamic vinegar and a little salt and pepper. Magic shortcut!

Love

ASPARAGUS

 SERVES 2 10 MINUTES 20 MINUTES

Certain foods like asparagus and artichokes possess so many benefits that they belong in many magical healing recipes. These vegetables–which both resemble flowers–can be used in detox spells, discernment spells, spells for the liver and digestive system, and spells for heart health. The soluble fiber in asparagus helps reduce the absorption of cholesterol into the blood. Asparagus is also rich in vitamin K, which supports blood flow and has anti-inflammatory and antioxidant properties that protect the heart. Artichokes have similar anti-inflammatory benefits but are also particularly high in polyphenols like quercetin, another antioxidant that supports heart health. Artichokes are also an excellent detox food and support the liver and kidneys in addition to helping balance cholesterol. We're focusing on heart health for this spell but be aware that it will bring you many other magical benefits.

FOR THE HEART VEGETABLES

- 1 BUNCH GREEN ASPARAGUS
- 1 TBSP OLIVE OIL
- SALT AND PEPPER
- 5 OZ (150 G) ARTICHOKE HEARTS (4 OR 5)

- 2 TSP BALSAMIC VINEGAR
- PINE NUTS, ROASTED
- PEPPER

FOR THE RASPBERRY VINAIGRETTE

- 3½ OZ (100 G) FROZEN RASPBERRIES
- 7 TBSP (10 CL) OF WATER
- 1 TBSP BALSAMIC VINEGAR
- SALT AND PEPPER

▽ Preheat the oven to 400°F (200°C).

THE HEART VEGETABLES

▽ Remove the tough stems from the asparagus spears, brush with olive oil, and sprinkle with salt and pepper. Place them on a greased baking tray. Cut the artichoke hearts in quarters and place them on the tray with the asparagus. Sprinkle with balsamic vinegar and bake for 15 minutes.

THE RASPBERRY VINAIGRETTE

▽ While the heart vegetables are in the oven, put the raspberries in a saucepan with 7 tbsp (10 cl) of water. Cook until defrosted. Pass the raspberries through a sieve, discard the seeds, and return the juice to the pan along with the vinegar, salt, and a good amount of pepper. Reduce the sauce until it is slightly thick.

▽ Remove the vegetables from the oven and drizzle with raspberry vinaigrette, then sprinkle with pine nuts (dry-roasted in a sauté pan for a few minutes ahead of time) and pepper.

Energetic
BUDDHA BOWL

 SERVES 2   15 MINUTES   🔲 30 MINUTES

This recipe is an homage to the meals of the Buddha, the master of enlightenment and eternal life. According to legend, during his life on earth, the Buddha brought his little bowl with him every-where he went, and people would give him what they could to eat. It was farmer's food—grains and steamed vegetables—but sometimes simple country food is much healthier than an elaborate diet. And in spite of certain artistic depictions, the Buddha was very thin during his human life. He later became a symbol of eternal life, and perhaps the secret to longevity is hidden in the Buddha bowl. My interpretation offers a rainbow of vegetables bringing together all the nutrients you need. Better still, thanks to the protein from the quinoa, the complex carbohydrates from the sweet potato, and beets that stimulate physical performance, this Buddha bowl offers not only the promise of a long life, but also a life full of energy!

- 5 OZ (150 G) QUINOA
- SALT
- 1 SWEET POTATO
- ½ BUNCH GREEN ASPARAGUS
- 3½ OZ (100 G) BRUSSELS SPROUTS
- 2 TSP OLIVE OIL
- ½ AVOCADO
- 2 COOKED BEETS
- A FEW HANDFULS OF LAMB'S LETTUCE
(OR ARUGULA OR BABY SPINACH)

- 2 OZ (50 G) BLUEBERRIES
- 2 TSP PUMPKIN SEEDS OR FLAX SEEDS

FOR THE LIME DRESSING

- JUICE OF ½ LIME
- 1 TSP WHITE BALSAMIC VINEGAR
- 1 TBSP OLIVE OIL
- ½ TSP MUSTARD
- SALT AND PEPPER

▽ Cook the quinoa in a pot of boiling water with a little salt for 15 minutes until the grains begin to sprout. Remove excess water. Peel the sweet potato, slice it, and cook in boiling water for 10 minutes.

▽ Remove about an inch of the tough aspara-gus stem. Remove the small stems and outermost leaves from the brussels sprouts and cut them in half. Heat the olive oil in a pan over high heat and sauté the asparagus and brussels sprouts until they start to brown.

▽ Dice the avocado and beets.

Place the lettuce in the bottom of two large bowls. Next add the hot quinoa, sweet potato, asparagus, and brussels sprouts (still hot!), followed by the avo-cado, beets, and blueberries.

THE LIME DRESSING
Mix together all of the dressing ingredients in a small bowl and dress the salad. Sprinkle with pump-kin seeds or flax seeds.

WITCH'S SECRET

What's so magical about the Buddha's diet? The endless combinations of vegetables and grains! To bring some variety to your energetic mixtures, try integrating other healing combinations like buckwheat and lentils with radishes, raspberries, cherry tomatoes, and walnuts.

Protection Chicken with Balsamic Sauce (see recipe on p. 66)

Air
RECIPES

$$\triangle$$

POULTRY
FOOD THAT FLIES

As we have seen in the first chapter, our life force comes from the earth. **But for a flavorful diet and optimal health, all four elements are indispensable. The air element abounds with nutritional benefits.** Poultry contains complete proteins, meaning all necessary amino acids (essential for several metabolic processes and for nervous system function), and B vitamins, which play many roles in our bodies, most notably in red blood cell production. These same characteristics are also found in certain vegetables, but in smaller quantities. To benefit the most from the air element, I suggest choosing organic, free-range poultry that has been raised in good conditions without antibiotic treatment. This kind of poultry is not only good for our health, but also for the health of the earth. Living like a witch means respecting the elements, plants, and animals that nourish the cycles of life.

Healing
WINTER CHICKEN

 SERVES 4   30 MINUTES.   1 HOUR–1 HOUR 30 MINUTES

If you have a mild illness or even if your immune system just needs a little boost, this chicken will offer you much more than just flavor. It is infused with ginger, an anti-inflammatory root that fights the common cold and supports the respiratory system. For this recipe, I also invoke the power of lemon to balance blood pH and to reinforce the immune system with its high level of vitamin C. The garlic adds antioxidants, increases immune defense, and fights cold and flu viruses. Healing herbs like rosemary, thyme, and parsley possess antiviral, antibacterial, and anti-inflammatory properties. This chicken is full of flavor and herbal magic and can be served on a bed of ginger-roasted broccoli rich in vitamin C and antioxidants to detoxify the body. Together, the benefits of these different elements combine to create a recipe for vitality and lightness that heals the body in profound ways whether you are sick or not.

- **1** HEAD BROCCOLI
- **4** SMALL ONIONS
- **4** GARLIC CLOVES, MINCED (KEEP THE SKIN), DIVIDED
- ½ OZ **(15** G) FRESH GINGER, GRATED, DIVIDED
- **3½** TBSP **(5** CL) OLIVE OIL, DIVIDED
- SALT AND PEPPER
- FRESH HERBS: PARSLEY, ROSEMARY, THYME
- JUICE OF **3** ORGANIC LEMONS (KEEP THE PEEL)
- **1** WHOLE FREE-RANGE CHICKEN

△ Preheat the oven to 375°F (190°C).

THE BROCCOLI

△ Divide the head of broccoli into small florets, then peel the onions and cut them in half or quarters depending on the size. Place them in a bowl and add half of the minced garlic, half of the ginger, peeled and crushed, half of the olive oil, and a little salt and pepper. Toss to make sure that the broccoli is thoroughly coated with the mixture. Transfer to a baking tray and top with a few sprigs of fresh herbs.

THE CHICKEN

△ Zest two of the lemons and set aside before extracting the juice, which will be added last. Place the garlic skin and lemon peels inside the chicken with a few sprigs and leaves of your fresh herbs as well as a teaspoon each of salt and pepper. What we put inside the chicken perfumes the meat even more than what we put on the outside.

△ Finely chop the remaining herbs. Mix together with the remaining minced garlic, oil, crushed ginger, and lemon zest and some salt and pepper. Cover the chicken with this aromatic oil.

△ Place the chicken on the bed of broccoli. Drizzle the whole thing with lemon juice and bake. Here's a rule of thumb for cooking a whole chicken: 25 minutes per 1 pound (about 500 g) of meat. Keep the bones to make a Bone Broth (p. 159). The bones can also be stored in the freezer for future broths.

WITCH'S SECRET

Rub oil or butter (mixed with herbs and garlic) under the bird's skin, not just on the surface. This cooking technique allows the seasoning to permeate the meat and gives an even crispier skin.

WITCH'S SECRET

You can also put the cauliflower directly in the sauce with the chicken rather than serve it as a separate dish. And for a more exotic flavor, add a small spoonful of curry powder and cumin to the sauce, or even a little ginger and turmeric for an extra anti-inflammatory immunity boost.

Soothing
CHICKEN

 SERVES 4 · 15 MINUTES · 20 MINUTES

Here's a chicken recipe with calming benefits for the body and mind. The B vitamins contained in poultry, vitamin B5 in particular, help regulate cortisol levels and reduce stress. But let's amplify these soothing effects by adding a healthy serving of coconut cream, which also contains vitamin B5. By mixing coconut cream with cashew cream (rich in magnesium), we can work on lowering physical stress. Magnesium is known for preserving nervous and muscular equilibrium and for protecting the body from anxiety and fatigue. Every ingredient in this spell offers soothing properties: walnut oil helps the body better adapt to stress and the cauliflower and sweet potato cream both contain vitamin C, which helps lower levels of the stress hormones.

FOR THE MUSTARD ROASTED CAULIFLOWER

- 1 HEAD CAULIFLOWER
- 5 TBSP (7 CL) OLIVE OIL
- 3½ TBSP (5 CL) BALSAMIC VINEGAR
- 1 TBSP MUSTARD
- 1 GARLIC CLOVE, MINCED
- SALT AND PEPPER

FOR THE CHICKEN WITH SWEET POTATO CREAM

- 1 LARGE SWEET POTATO
- 2 ONIONS
- 1 TBSP WALNUT OIL
- 1 GARLIC CLOVE, MINCED
- 7 TBSP (10 CL) COCONUT CREAM
- 7 TBSP (10 CL) CASHEW CREAM
- 3–4 THYME SPRIGS
- SALT AND PEPPER
- 17½ OZ (500 G) FREE-RANGE CHICKEN CUTLETS
- BUTTER OR OIL FOR COOKING

△ Preheat the oven to 400°F (200°C).

THE MUSTARD CAULIFLOWER

△ Divide the cauliflower into small florets. In a large bowl, whisk together all of the ingredients for the sauce: oil, vinegar, mustard, minced garlic, salt, and pepper. Add the cauliflower and coat well. Transfer the florets to a baking tray and bake for around 20 minutes or until they start to brown on the outside and are tender on the inside.

THE CHICKEN WITH SWEET POTATO CREAM

△ Peel and slice the sweet potato and the onions. Sauté in a pan with the walnut oil and minced garlic until tender. Next add the coconut cream and cashew cream (you can make your own cashew cream by blending together raw cashews with a splash of water until smooth and creamy), thyme leaves, salt, and pepper. When the cream has reduced and thickened after about 10 minutes, remove from heat and use an immersion blender to blend it into a smooth sauce. For a sauce with more texture, you can also just mash the vegetables with a spoon.

△ Cut the chicken into chunks or slices. Sauté over high heat with a little oil or butter until all of the chicken begins to brown on the outside. Then, transfer the chicken to the pan with the sweet potato cream and cook for 5 more minutes.

△ Serve the chicken and sweet potato cream sauce with the cauliflower and a few thyme sprigs.

Euphoria Turkey
WITH RASPBERRY SAUCE

 SERVES 4 30 MINUTES. 40 MINUTES

Chocolate isn't the only food that can make people happy—berries and air recipes can, too! All poultry contains anti-stress properties, but turkey is particularly rich in tryptophan, an amino acid that is the precursor of serotonin, the happiness hormone. The lentils that are served with it help increase serotonin production thanks to their complex carbohydrates and high levels of folate (vitamin B9), which may protect from symptoms of depression. Berries also possess this power: They are filled with antioxidants, boost dopamine production in the brain, and are also, like lentils, rich in folate. Berries can even maximize the effects of tryptophan. The combination of turkey, raspberries soaked in red wine and perfumed with rosemary, and lentils infused with turkey drippings is so delicious that it is impossible for this spell to make you anything but happy.

FOR THE RASPBERRY SAUCE

- 21 oz (600 g) FROZEN RASPBERRIES
- 3½ TBSP (5 cL) RED WINE
- 2 TSP BALSAMIC VINEGAR
- 2 TSP OLIVE OIL
- 2 TSP HONEY
- 2 ROSEMARY SPRIGS, VERY FINELY MINCED
- SALT AND PEPPER

FOR THE TURKEY WITH LENTILS

- 9 oz (250 g) RED LENTILS
- A FEW ROSEMARY SPRIGS
- SALT AND PEPPER
- 2 TBSP SUNFLOWER OR OLIVE OIL
- 17½–21 oz (500–600 g) TURKEY CUTLETS

△ Preheat the oven to 400°F (200°C).

THE RASPBERRY SAUCE

△ Place the frozen raspberries in a small pot. Add a few spoonsful of water and let them defrost. Crush them using a spoon and press them through a sieve to extract the juice. Add the raspberry juice back to the pot, followed by the other ingredients for the sauce. Let the sauce reduce over low heat for a few minutes. Set aside.

THE TURKEY WITH LENTILS

△ Cook the lentils in a pot of boiling water with leaves from 1 rosemary sprig and a little salt and pepper for 15 minutes.

△ Heat the oil in a large pan over high heat. Season the turkey cutlets with salt and pepper and place them in the pan. Cook for 2 minutes on each side.

△ Transfer the lentils to a baking dish and place the cutlets on top along with a few rosemary sprigs. Add a few spoonsful of raspberry sauce on top of the turkey. Bake for 15 minutes. Serve warm with a few fresh rosemary sprigs and a few more spoonsful of warm raspberry sauce. Transfer the rest of the raspberry sauce to a sauce dish on the table.

WITCH'S SECRET

To make the lentils easier to digest, soak them in water overnight before cooking them. And if you don't have time to prepare the raspberry juice yourself, you can buy a pre-made raspberry coulis and add the wine, balsamic vinegar, olive oil, and rosemary.

Immunity
ORANGE DUCK

 SERVES 4  15 MINUTES. 30 MINUTES

For this spell, we're flipping the classic orange duck recipe: instead of putting the orange on the bird, we're going to put the bird *inside* the orange. Duck is misunderstood: it is often not considered a healthy food and when we think of duck fat we think of rich and indulgent eating. And yet, it actually holds various health benefits. Not all fats are created equal, and duck fat is closer to olive oil than butter. In addition, this poultry is very rich in protein (which strengthens the immune system) and contains even more iron than chicken. It is also an excellent source of minerals like zinc and selenium, which also promote healthy immune system function. This duck is cooked inside an orange full of vitamin C to amplify its powers of defense. We also are using the whole orange because vitamin C and antioxidants are even more concentrated in the peel. Immunity-boosting cinnamon and star anise are the perfect accompaniment for these ingredients, as are figs, which contain a substance that calms throat discomfort. If you are treating or preventing a winter illness, I suggest preparing these little stuffed oranges for a culinary delight that is also charged with healing magic.

- 4 ORGANIC ORANGES
- 3½ OZ (100 G) DRIED FIGS
- 2¼–3 OZ (60–80 G) DRIED CRANBERRIES, CHOPPED

- 7 TBSP (10 CL) RED WINE
- ⅙ OZ (5 G) HONEY
- 1 CINNAMON STICK
- 3 STAR ANISE PODS

- SALT AND PEPPER
- 1 APPLE
- 7 OZ (200 G) SLICED DUCK BREAST

△ Preheat the oven to 350°F (180°C).

△ Cut off the top of each orange. Remove the pulp using a spoon, then blend it into a puree and press it through a fine sieve. You can also use a citrus juicer, but be careful not to break the skin. Collect the juice and put it in a small saucepan.

△ Chop the figs and cook them in the orange juice over low heat with the cranberries, wine, honey, cinnamon, star anise, and a pinch of salt and pepper for 5 minutes.

△ Peel and slice the apple into small cubes and cook them with the orange-fig sauce until you have a fairly thick filling. Remove the star anise pods and cinnamon stick.

△ Slice the duck into small pieces. Mix with the fruit filling and spoon this preparation into the emptied oranges. Put the tops back on the oranges and bake for 20–25 minutes.

WITCH'S SECRET

To make this recipe even easier and more flavorful, you can prepare the recipe the night before, store them in the refrigerator, and cook the stuffed oranges just before serving. You can also freeze them before cooking. Just let them defrost in the refrigerator before cooking as described in the recipe. The fruit filling will act like a marinade and give the duck even more flavor.

Crispy Craving CHICKEN

 SERVES 2 20 MINUTES. 30–40 MINUTES

Sometimes we crave certain fast foods. Like fried chicken and potato chips. Very often, these cravings come from a need for energy in the form of carbohydrates and fat, which is essential for brain function and energy production. There is a way to satisfy these cravings while still nourishing the body in the right way. Using almond flour and shredded coconut to bread the chicken is not only more flavorful than flour-based breading, it also offers energy renewal that is amplified by the protein in the chicken. The nutrient-dense veggie chips provide a good dose of complex carbohydrates that balance blood sugar levels and offer long-term energy. Magic and delicious!

FOR THE VEGGIE CHIPS

- 1 SWEET POTATO
- 1 EGGPLANT
- 1 ZUCCHINI
- 4–5½ TBSP (6–8 CL) OLIVE OIL
- SALT AND PEPPER

FOR THE CRISPY CHICKEN

- 2 OZ (50 G) ALMOND FLOUR
- 2 OZ (50 G) SHREDDED COCONUT
- SALT AND PEPPER
- 2 EGGS, WHISKED
- 14 OZ (400 G) CHICKEN CUTLETS

FOR THE HONEY MUSTARD SAUCE

- 3½ OZ (100 G) YOGURT
- ⅓ OZ (10 G) MUSTARD
- 1 OZ (30 G) HONEY
- SALT AND PEPPER

△ Preheat the oven to 400°F (200°C).

THE VEGGIE CHIPS

△ Peel and thinly slice the sweet potato, eggplant, and zucchini. Thoroughly coat the vegetables in olive oil and sprinkle with salt and pepper. Arrange them on a baking tray lined with parchment paper and set aside.

THE CRISPY CHICKEN

△ Mix together the almond flour, shredded coconut, salt, and pepper in a shallow bowl. Beat the eggs in a separate dish.

△ Dip the chicken cutlets in the whisked eggs, then in the almond-coconut mixture. Make sure each side is coated. Repeat this step a second time for extra crunch.

△ Place the cutlets on the baking tray with the veggie chips and bake for 10 minutes. Turn the chicken cutlets and veggie chips over and continue baking for about 10 minutes until the chips and the chicken are crispy.

THE HONEY MUSTARD SAUCE

△ Place all of the ingredients for the sauce in a bowl and mix thoroughly.

△ Serve the chicken with the veggie chips and the honey mustard sauce on the side.

WITCH'S SECRET

For an even tastier version you can fry the chicken, but make sure you use a good oil like organic grapeseed oil, which is neutral, nontoxic, and has a high burning point.

Forest
QUAIL

 SERVES 4   10 MINUTES.   10 MINUTES

When it comes to food, size isn't everything! **Some of the smallest ingredients can contain even more nutrients than larger ones.** You might be surprised to learn that a tiny quail has higher concentrations of protein and B vitamins per gram than turkey, and the same is true for quail eggs. There is also considerably more iron in one portion of quail than in an equivalent portion of chicken. This is particularly advantageous for people with digestive problems who have to reduce their meal sizes, who are on a diet, or who need to regain their strength after an illness. To amplify the benefits of this forest recipe, I'm adding shiitake mushrooms, which are packed with vitamin D and minerals. For such a little mushroom, the shiitake offers a big dose of this immunostimulant vitamin. Blackberries are also particularly rich in antioxidants, more so than other berries, as seen in their dark purple color. And there's a reason the shiitake, little yellow onions, and blackberries caramelized in balsamic vinegar go so well with quail. This combination is as flavorful as it is good for your health.

- **8** PEARL ONIONS
- **5** OZ **(150** G) BLACKBERRIES, DIVIDED
- **4–6** WHOLE QUAIL
- SALT AND PEPPER

- **1** BUNCH THYME, DIVIDED
- **1** TBSP OLIVE OIL
- **7** OZ **(200** G) SHIITAKE AND BUTTON MUSHROOMS

- **7** TBSP **(10** CL) BALSAMIC VINEGAR
- **7** TBSP **(10** CL) RED WINE
- SEEDS OF **1** POMEGRANATE

△ Preheat the oven to 400°F (200°C).

△ Peel the onions and cut the larger ones in half. Place half of an onion and 1 or 2 blackberries inside each quail along with salt, pepper, and a thyme sprig to perfume the meat.

△ Place the quail in a baking dish, drizzle with olive oil, and sprinkle with salt and pepper. Arrange the shiitake and button mushrooms (whole or in pieces if they are large), the onions and the rest of the blackberries and thyme sprigs around the quail.

△ Drizzle everything with a little more olive oil, the balsamic vinegar and wine, and sprinkle with salt and pepper. You can also put a small spoonful of vinegar and a little wine inside the quail to add more flavor to the meat.

△ Bake for 10 minutes. Add a few fresh thyme sprigs and pomegranate seeds before serving.

△ Keep the quail bones (even in the freezer if you don't have time right away) to make broths and soup bases, like the Bone Broth (p. 159).

WITCH'S
SECRET

To surprise your guests,
place a quail egg inside
each little bird!

WITCH'S SECRET

Deglaze the leeks several times during cooking (or as soon as they start sticking to the pan) to extract their liquid and encourage caramelization. As soon as the leek liquid is absorbed, add 1 spoonful of water. Repeat this process until the leeks are sufficiently browned and caramelized.

Comfort
CHICKEN

 SERVES 4 20 MINUTES. 40 MINUTES

Sometimes we just need comforting recipes—ones that taste like someone's grandmother made them, ones that warm the body and the soul. But comforting meals don't have to be overly rich. This grilled chicken with leek cream sauce accompanied by stuffed mushrooms not only contains good protein and essential vitamins, it also has an incredible flavor. The cream and cheese, a little rich but not without their own health benefits, are balanced by the chicken, leeks, and mushrooms, which are low in calories. The magic is in the way this recipe brings together pleasure, comfort, and well-being . . .

FOR THE LEEK CREAM SAUCE

- **2** LEEKS
- **4** TSP SUNFLOWER OR OLIVE OIL
- **13½** FL OZ **(40** CL) ORGANIC CRÈME FRAÎCHE (OR COCONUT CREAM OR SOUR CREAM)
- SALT AND PEPPER

FOR THE STUFFED MUSHROOMS

- **17½** OZ **(500** G) BUTTON MUSHROOMS
- **3½** OZ **(100** G) BLUE CHEESE (OR ANY CHEESE OF YOUR CHOOSING)

FOR THE CHICKEN

- **17½** OZ **(500** G) FREE-RANGE CHICKEN CUTLETS
- SALT AND PEPPER
- **1** TBSP OLIVE OIL
- RICE, LENTILS, OR VEGETABLES FOR SERVING

△ Preheat the oven to 350°F (180°C).

THE LEEK CREAM SAUCE

△ Remove the green part of the leeks (keep it for Bone Broth, page 159) and slice the white part into quarter-inch rounds. Heat the oil in a pan over medium heat and add the leeks. Cook them for 15–20 minutes until they are completely caramelized. Incorporate the cream and a little salt and pepper (you might want to try doubling the amount of pepper for this recipe—you won't regret it!) and let the sauce reduce for 10 more minutes over low heat.

THE STUFFED MUSHROOMS

Remove the mushroom stems and hollow out the caps (you can keep the stems and extra flesh for other recipes like the Immunity Mushroom Quiche p. 16). Fill them with cheese and bake on a tray for 10 minutes.

THE CHICKEN

△ While the leek cream sauce is reducing and the mushrooms baking, cut the chicken into small 1- to 2-inch pieces. Season with salt and pepper. Heat the oil in a pan over high heat. Cook the chicken, stirring often, until the pieces are lightly browned on all sides.

△ Mix the chicken with the sauce to allow all of the flavors to combine and serve alone or with rice, lentils, or other vegetables with the stuffed mushrooms on the side.

Slimming Turkey
ROULADES

 SERVES 4  20 MINUTES. 35 MINUTES

To lower cholesterol or even to lose weight, you have to eat the right foods. Certain foods help the body manage fat, sugar, and cholesterol better than others. This is particularly true for turkey, prunes, walnuts, and chestnuts. The protein in turkey helps you feel satiated and facilitates muscle repair (which helps burn fat) and turkey is also low in fat, cholesterol, and calories. Prunes cooked in wine also satiate the body and provide antioxidants. Like prunes, the walnuts and chestnuts in the stuffing are full of fiber that slows the absorption of cholesterol into the blood, and the healthy oil in the walnuts stimulates the body to burn fat instead of storing it. To maintain a good cholesterol level and a healthy weight, slimming culinary spells like these turkey roulades are an excellent solution that is healthy and indulgent.

FOR THE TURKEY ROULADES

- 2 ONIONS
- 1 OZ (30 G) WALNUTS
- 3½ OZ (100 G) COOKED CHESTNUTS
- 2 TBSP OLIVE OIL

- SALT AND PEPPER
- 17½–21 OZ (500–600 G) TURKEY CUTLETS

FOR THE PRUNE AND WINE SAUCE

- 1 GARLIC CLOVE
- 1 SHALLOT
- 3½ OZ (100 G) PITTED PRUNES
- 6¾ FL OZ (20 CL) RED WINE
- 7 TBSP (10 CL) OF WATER

△ Preheat the oven to 350°F (180°C).

THE TURKEY ROULADES

△ Peel and finely chop the onions. Finely chop the walnuts and chestnuts. Sauté the onions in a large pan with the oil until they are tender and browned, about 10 minutes (add a splash of water to deglaze). Add the walnuts, chestnuts, and a little salt and pepper. Let cook for a few more minutes.

△ Use a meat tenderizer to flatten the turkey cutlets as much as you can. Spread the onion and nut stuffing evenly over each cutlet and roll them up tight. Place them one at a time in a baking dish, making sure the opening of the roll is touching the bottom of the pan, to prevent them from unraveling. Season with salt and pepper and bake for 20 minutes.

THE PRUNE AND WINE SAUCE

△ Peel and finely chop the garlic and shallot. Combine all of the sauce ingredients in a small saucepan with 7 tbsp (10 cl) of water and cook for at least 20 minutes over low heat while the roulades are cooking. Blend the sauce into a puree with an immersion blender. If the sauce is still too thick, add a few spoonsful of water.

△ Remove the roulades from the oven and serve them covered with the prune and wine sauce.

WITCH'S SECRET

There are many other magical ingredients not used in this spell that also lower cholesterol. Red rice yeast, oily fish, garlic, and hibiscus, for example, all work to block bad cholesterol. So many natural and safe solutions exist—you just have to know where to look. And that is what witches do best!

Protection Chicken
WITH BALSAMIC SAUCE

 SERVES 4 10 MINUTES. 40 MINUTES

In today's world, protective spells are more necessary than ever. Modern life exposes us to many pollutants. I am referring to the traces of toxic chemical products that are found in almost everything we eat, the hormones given to livestock, heavy metals in fish, pesticides in soil and air pollution, and stress in general. All of this creates oxidation and is therefore harmful to the body. But there are incredibly effective spells that can protect us from these attacks. The magic ingredient? Antioxidants. Vitamins C, E, and A are just a few examples, and certain foods like onions (especially red onions), garlic, and balsamic vinegar, which also helps digestion, contain particularly high levels of antioxidants. There's a reason these ingredients go so well together!

- 17½ OZ (500 G) FREE-RANGE CHICKEN CUTLETS OR THIGHS
- 6¾ FL OZ (20 CL) BALSAMIC VINEGAR
- 5–6 GARLIC CLOVES, DIVIDED
- SALT AND PEPPER
- 4–5 RED ONIONS
- 1 TBSP SUNFLOWER OR OLIVE OIL

△ Preheat the oven to 400°F (200°C).

△ Put the chicken in a dish to marinate with the balsamic vinegar, 2 minced garlic cloves, salt, and pepper, while you prepare the onions.

△ Peel the onions and cut them into quarters. Heat half of the oil in a pan (one that can go in the oven, if you have it) and add the onions, cut-side up, as well as the rest of the garlic (whole, with peel). Then pour in the rest of the oil. Season with salt and pepper. Cover the pan and cook for 15–20 minutes over medium heat.

△ Next, add the chicken to the pan of onions along with half of the chicken marinade. If you don't have an oven-safe pan, transfer the onions and chicken to a baking dish. Add a final pinch of salt and pepper and bake for 15–20 minutes.

WITCH'S SECRET

You can replace the chicken with beef or veal. And for a vegetarian version, I suggest cauliflower or broccoli florets. The vitamin C and other antioxidants present in the vegetables will make this spell even more powerful! If you have sauce left over, freeze it for other recipes.

Turkey
FOR SLEEP

  SERVES 2 15 MINUTES. 30 MINUTES

We saw in the spell for Euphoria Turkey (p. 56) that this air creature is loaded with tryptophan, which promotes tranquility and joy. But we can also use the magic of this food to provoke a gentle sleepiness if combined with the right ingredients. Welcome to molecular magic! The tryptophan contained in turkey helps with the production of serotonin, the precursor of melatonin, the sleep hormone. But tryptophan needs calcium to adequately produce serotonin. So, we're adding vegetables that are rich in calcium, like spinach, lentils, and soy cream as well as a feta (which contains even more calcium) to amplify tryptophan's potential. The result? Serotonin production, which means more melatonin and a deeper sleep. And if you need a little something extra to help you dream more easily, I suggest the Dreamland Potion (p. 151).

- 9 oz (250 g) LENTILS
- SALT AND PEPPER
- 7 oz (200 g) FRESH SPINACH
- 8½ FL oz (25 CL) SOY CREAM

- 14–17½ oz (400–500 g) TURKEY
- 1 TBSP OLIVE OIL
- ¾ oz (20 g) BUTTER
- 3½ oz (100 g) FETA

△ Cook the lentils in a pot of water or in a pan for 15–20 minutes. When the lentils are cooked and all of the water is absorbed, season with salt and pepper and add the spinach and soy cream. Let this mixture reduce over low heat for around 5 minutes.

△ Cut the turkey into small pieces and grill in a pan with the olive oil and butter until browned on all sides. Add the turkey to the warm lentils and spinach, and top with crumbled feta.

△ Serve warm with a drizzle of olive oil and some pepper.

WITCH'S SECRET

To multiply the effects of tryptophan and calcium, you can marinate the turkey in an organic milk bath before cooking it. This will infuse the poultry with the good calcium found in dairy products and render the meat even more tender.

Duck Tart for Fighting
THE FIRES OF INFLAMMATION

  SERVES 4 20 MINUTES. 20–30 MINUTES

Perhaps you've heard the phrase, "Inflammation is the cause of all disease." All right, so we have to fight it. But what exactly is inflammation? Basically, it's a series of immune system defense mechanisms that heat the body. Inflammation is like an invisible fire inside your body. And having too much fire can damage organs and promote disease. But not all inflammation is bad. Think of fevers while fighting a virus and bug bite rashes. These reactions are part of the healing process, and we all need some level of inflammation, but we need just the right balance. You should always look for the root cause of inflammation, but food can help calm this defense reaction when it goes into overdrive. Shallots, onions, sweet potatoes, pears, and even duck have anti-inflammatory properties. Duck is high in monounsaturated fat, a healthy fat like those found in olive oil that fights inflammatory fires in the body. A duck tart with caramelized shallots makes the idea of an "anti-inflammatory" diet much more inviting!

- 9 OZ **(250 G)** SHALLOTS, DIVIDED
- 1 RED ONION
- 1 PEAR

- 2 TBSP OLIVE OIL
- 3½ TBSP **(5 CL)** ORGANIC CRÈME FRAÎCHE (OR COCONUT CREAM OR SOUR CREAM)

- 1 SWEET POTATO
- 5 OZ **(150 G)** DUCK BREAST
- 3½ TBSP **(5 CL)** BALSAMIC VINEGAR

⊿ Preheat the oven to 350°F (180°C).

⊿ Set aside 5 or 6 shallots to caramelize in balsamic vinegar to decorate the tart. Peel and finely chop the rest of the shallots, onion, and pear, and let them slowly cook in a pan with the olive oil until soft. When they start sticking to the pan, add a few spoonsful of water to deglaze the pan and scrape any pieces from the bottom of the pan with a spatula. Let them continue to caramelize over low heat for around 5 more minutes.

⊿ When they seem crispy yet tender enough, incorporate the crème fraîche, mix, and reduce.

⊿ Peel the sweet potato and slice it as thinly as possible. You can also use a mandoline. Grease a tart pan and arrange the sweet potato slices in concentric overlapping circles along the base and the sides

⊿ To make the decoration, peel the shallots you set aside earlier and place them in a saucepan. Cover with water and add the balsamic vinegar. Let the shallots boil until the vinegar water is completely absorbed and the only liquid remaining is a thick balsamic vinegar caramel. Stir gently and remove from heat once the onions are fully coated with the caramel glaze. Set aside.

⊿ Pour the shallot cream into the sweet potato crust. Slice the duck and arrange on top of the shallots. Bake the tart for 20–30 minutes.

⊿ After removing the tart from the oven, arrange the caramelized shallots on top and serve warm.

WITCH'S SECRET

Want to increase the anti-inflammatory magic of this spell? Replace the duck with salmon or cod and bake the tart in the same way. The healthy anti-inflammatory fats in the fish will amplify the vegetables' protective effects.

WITCH'S SECRET

One of the most overlooked steps of cooking meat is letting it properly rest before serving. Remove the chicken from the oven, cover the pot with a lid, leaving a little room for steam to escape, and let it rest for 20-30 minutes. The juices that escaped from the chicken during cooking will be reabsorbed during this rest period, along with the coconut sauce, rendering the chicken even juicier.

Satisfaction CHICKEN

SERVES 4 · 10 MINUTES + 40 MINUTES (MARINADE) · 1 HOUR–1 HOUR 30 MINUTES

Do you ever feel like you're always hungry? Like nothing can suppress your desire to eat, and nothing really satisfies you? When we feel this way, we often turn to unhealthy options, and then our hunger can turn to nausea. It's terrible, but there is a remedy for this (and a way to prevent it) and it comes in the form of a satiety chicken spell. This chicken is stuffed with nourishing protein and cooked in coconut cream, a healthy fat that helps you feel full—just like the complex carbohydrates in sweet potatoes that take longer to digest and help balance blood sugar. We're also going to add some cayenne pepper and ginger to boost metabolism. And our final magic satisfaction ingredient? Pine nuts, which contain fat that tells your brain when you are full. Very often, an insatiable desire to eat something is actually a lack of certain nutrients . . . and a lack of culinary magic!

- 5 SMALL (OR 2–3 LARGE) SWEET POTATOES
- 2–3 APPLES
- 8 SHALLOTS
- ⅓ OZ (10 G) FRESH GINGER

- 20 FL OZ (60 CL) COCONUT CREAM
- ¼ TSP CAYENNE PEPPER
- 4 TSP WHITE BALSAMIC VINEGAR OR LEMON JUICE
- SALT AND PEPPER

- 1 WHOLE FREE-RANGE CHICKEN
- 3½ OZ (100 G) PINE NUTS, DRY-ROASTED

△ Peel and slice the sweet potatoes and apples. Peel the shallots and grate the ginger. Pour the coconut cream into a large oven-safe pot and add the sweet potatoes, apples, and whole shallots. Then add the ginger, cayenne pepper, white balsamic vinegar, salt, and pepper. Mix well. Place the whole chicken in this satiety bath and let it marinate away from the heat for at least 20 minutes on each side.

△ Preheat the oven to 375°F (190°C).

△ Roast the chicken, breast-side up, for 1 hour to 1 hour, 30 minutes depending on its size. (The golden rule for cooking a whole chicken? 25 minutes per each pound [about 500 g] of meat.)

△ Serve this chicken sprinkled with dry-roasted pine nuts.

Aztec Awakening
CHICKEN

 SERVES 4–6   🕐 20 MIN.   🔲 55 MINUTES TO 1 HOUR

Chocolate is a pretty magical healing ingredient. But did you know that it's also a symbol of wisdom? The Aztecs were the first to use cacao beans. They believed these beans came from the gods and that humans could receive wisdom by drinking spiced hot chocolate. Thinking of chocolate as just a candy is underestimating its immense power. Chocolate reduces inflammation, is filled with antioxidants, and thanks to its high levels of magnesium, is also good for memory and concentration. By marrying chocolate with other ingredients that support brain function, like blood-flow-stimulating beets, ginger, chestnuts and rosemary, we can create a spell that satisfies both our mind and our palate with its unusual and seductive flavors.

FOR THE CHICKEN

- 6 RAW BEETS
- 3 RED ONIONS
- 3½ OZ (100 G) COOKED CHESTNUTS
- 2 TBSP OIL, DIVIDED
- SALT AND PEPPER

- 21–28 OZ (600–800 G) CHICKEN THIGHS
- 1 ROSEMARY SPRIG
- ¾ OZ (20 G) BUTTER

FOR THE AZTEC CHOCOLATE SAUCE

- ⅓ OZ (10 G) FRESH GINGER
- 2–3 ROSEMARY SPRIGS

- ¾ OZ (20 G) DARK CHOCOLATE (70% CACAO MINIMUM)
- 6¾ FL OZ (20 CL) COCONUT CREAM
- ⅛ TSP CHILI PEPPER
- 2 TBSP SUNFLOWER OR OLIVE OIL
- 7 TBSP (10 CL) OF WATER

△ Preheat the oven to 400°F (200°C).

THE CHICKEN

△ Peel and slice the beets into quarters and the onions in half. Place them on a baking tray lined with parchment paper along with the whole chestnuts. Drizzle with half of the oil and season with salt and pepper. Cover the baking tray with aluminum foil, then bake for around 30 minutes until you can pierce the beets with a knife.

△ While the vegetables are in the oven, season the chicken thighs with salt and pepper. Heat the rest of the oil in a pan over high heat with the rosemary leaves. Place the chicken in the pan. Then add the butter. Cook the thighs for 2–3 minutes on each side.

△ Remove the tray from the oven, place the chicken thighs on top of the beets and onions, and return it to the oven. Continue cooking for 20–25 more minutes.

THE AZTEC CHOCOLATE SAUCE

△ Peel and grate the ginger, remove the rosemary leaves. Melt the chocolate in a double boiler, (au bain marie), then incorporate the other ingredients along with 7 tbsp (10 cl) of water. Mix thoroughly, then let the sauce rest on the lowest heat while the chicken is in the oven.

△ Pour the sauce through a sieve. If it is too thick, add a few spoonsful of water.

△ Serve the chicken and vegetables covered with the Aztec sauce.

WITCH'S SECRET

To give the Aztec sauce an even deeper flavor, add 3½ tbsp (5 cl) of red wine. The antioxidants in red wine also help concentration, as long as you don't overindulge . . .

MACKEREL FOR MELANCHOLY (SEE RECIPE ON P. 83)

Water
RECIPES

FISH AND SHELLFISH
FOOD THAT COMES FROM THE SEA

Water contains a very subtle magic that is nevertheless extremely powerful. Whereas foods from the earth are becoming poorer and poorer in nutrients, this water element has an astonishing ability to maintain its virtues. Meat and poultry are too often filled with hormones and raised in cruel conditions. But foods from the water seem to have better luck: their precious nutrients are more preserved, and so are their trace minerals, which are found in lower quantities in elements from the earth. Fish and shellfish are not only filled with minerals like iron and zinc and vitamins B and D, they are also rich in EPA and DHA, a kind of omega-3 fatty acid, a healing fat, that is only found in marine fat sources. Eating fish lowers inflammation levels, reinforces heart and brain health, immune system function, and, truly, the entire body. But the ocean's magic is under threat: Water is becoming more and more polluted, the worldwide demand for fish is too great, the ocean food chain is out of balance, and water animals are dying as a result of climate change and pollution. Protecting the earth and oceans is everyone's responsibility. Fish is very good for our health, but we have to make sure that what is good for us is also good for our planet. The impact of every single person matters. The expression "'it's just a straw!' said 8 billion people" says it all. And these straws will end up in landfills and oceans. How can we save our planet? By prioritizing foods that come from the earth, limiting our consumption of meat to the essential, and choosing the right kinds of fish. What are the best water foods to eat that respect the environment? Here's my list: anchovies, sardines, all shellfish, Atlantic mackerel, Alaskan salmon, and albacore tuna. Living like a witch isn't only about practicing culinary spells to heal yourself. It also means taking responsibility for the earth and our food resources.

Immunity

SALMON

 SERVES 4 10 MINUTES 15 MINUTES

When we practice culinary magic, we discover combinations that are unusual but incredible. Salmon, cooked gently over a bed of fresh blueberries and shiitake mushrooms with a lemon and ginger broth, offers an inspired eating experience. Imagine delicate flavors, a perfect balance between the richness of the salmon and the sweetness of the shiitake, with little explosions of freshness from the blueberries. And while you're enjoying your meal, the magical ingredients in this recipe are working to boost your immunity. Salmon increases immune defense thanks to its vitamin D, and shiitake mushrooms (exceptionally rich in this vitamin compared to other earth elements) do the same. It's no surprise that both of them go wonderfully with blueberries, which are endowed with true protective powers. The antioxidants in these little berries work in tandem with vitamin D to maximize immune system function.

- 3½ TBSP (5 CL) OLIVE OIL, DIVIDED
- ⅙ OZ (5 G) FRESH GINGER, GRATED
- JUICE AND ZEST OF ½ LEMON
- 1 TSP HONEY
- SALT AND PEPPER
- 4 ORGANIC SALMON FILLETS
- 7–10½ OZ (200–300 G) FRESH BLUEBERRIES
- 3½ OZ (100 G) SHIITAKE MUSHROOMS

▽ Preheat the oven to 425°F (220°C).

▽ Pour half of the oil into the bottom of a baking dish. Mix the rest of the oil with the grated ginger, lemon zest, honey, salt, and pepper in a separate dish. Place the salmon fillets in the baking dish and cover with the mixture, making sure they are thoroughly coated. Arrange the blueberries and shiitake mushrooms around the fillets. If the mushrooms are large, you can slice them. Pour over the lemon juice.

▽ Bake for 12–15 minutes. Serve this dish with a garnish of few fresh blueberries for an extra explosion of fresh flavor.

WITCH'S SECRET

Do you want to maximize the immune benefits of this spell? Add a few spoonsful of Immunity Berry Syrup (p. 167) before cooking the dish. This potion is prepared with one of the most magical immunity ingredients.

Mermaid
SALAD

 SERVES 4   10 MINUTES   5 MINUTES

Some health secrets are hidden in the ocean's depths, and only mermaids and witches know about them. Trace elements (like iron, zinc, selenium, fluorine, chromium, copper, and iodine) are more easily found in shellfish and algae than in earth's vegetables. Legend says that mermaids don't age the way humans do. Perhaps their diets plays a role... Shellfish also contain lower levels of heavy metals than larger fish that are impacted by biomagnification. Algae, in this recipe, helps rid the body of toxins and protects the body from free radical damage and premature aging. This ocean salad also reinforces energy and is a good source of protein, omega-3s, and other nutrients that protect and detoxify the body. We could learn a lot from the way the mermaids eat.

- 2 TSP OLIVE OIL
- ½ GARLIC CLOVE, FINELY MINCED
- 5 OZ (150 G) BABY OCTOPUS (FRESH OR IN A PREMADE SALAD)
- 5⅓–7 OZ (150–200 G) COCKLES

- 7 OZ (200 G) BAY SCALLOPS
- 2 TBSP WHITE WINE
- SALT AND PEPPER
- 3½ OZ (100 G) FRESH ALGAE (WAKAME OR SEA SPAGHETTI)

- JUICE AND ZEST OF ½ ORGANIC LEMON
- 2¾–3½ OZ (80–100 G) SALMON (OR TROUT) ROE

▽ Heat the oil in a pan over high heat. Add the minced garlic and cook for 1 minute. Next add the baby octopus, cockles, and scallops and immediately pour in the white wine. Season with salt and pepper. Let cook, stirring with a wooden spoon, for 2–3 minutes until the shells open. Quickly remove the pan from the heat. Transfer the shellfish to another bowl to stop them from cooking.

▽ In a large bowl, combine the algae (thoroughly washed to remove any salt) and lemon juice and zest. Add the shellfish and stir everything together. Serve this salad on small plates or in the scallop shells and decorate with salmon roe just before serving.

WITCH'S SECRET

I think integrating more algae into your diet is great for everyone. It's a superfood packed with vitamins and minerals that support the thyroid and immune system, and aquatic vegetables are an excellent source of antioxidants and fiber that are fantastic for the heart and digestive system. Not at all high in calories, algae is also a good choice for the environment.

Relaxing Cod
BOULETTES

 **SERVES 4** 20 MINUTES 🔲 20 MINUTES

Why not take advantage of the magic of chamomile flowers in more than just a tea, but in a dinner recipe to calm you and give you better sleep? These cod boulettes are cooked in a cream infused with chamomile flowers that soothe the nervous and muscular systems and possess anti-inflammatory and immunostimulant properties. Lemon, which balances the richness of the cream, also contributes to healthy nervous system function because of its high potassium levels. Interestingly, anxiety can be linked to low levels of potassium. This recipe is easier than it looks, and you can pre-pare the boulettes ahead of time and freeze them to make sure you always have a spell on hand that promises a tranquil evening.

FOR THE BOULETTES

- **7** OZ **(200** G**)** COD
- **2** TBSP OLIVE OIL, DIVIDED
- **¾** OZ **(20** G**)** ALMOND FLOUR
- ZEST OF **1** ORGANIC LEMON
- SALT AND PEPPER

FOR THE CHAMOMILE-LEMON CREAM SAUCE

- **6¾** FL OZ **(20** CL**)** ORGANIC CRÈME FRAÎCHE (OR ORGANIC SOUR CREAM OR FULL-FAT YOGURT)
- JUICE OF **½** LEMON
- ZEST OF **1** ORGANIC LEMON
- **⅛** OZ **(5** G**)** DRIED CHAMOMILE FLOWERS
- SALT AND PEPPER

THE BOULETTES

▽ Lightly cook the cod in a pan over medium heat with half of the olive oil for 2–3 minutes. Break the fish into small chunks using a spatula during cook-ing. Transfer the fish to a large bowl and add the almond flour, lemon zest, salt, and pepper. Mix thor-oughly. Take one spoonful of the mixture at a time and form small balls with your hands.

▽ Cook the boulettes in a pan with the remaining oil until they are cooked on all sides.

THE CHAMOMILE-LEMON CREAM SAUCE

▽ Place all of the ingredients for the cream sauce in a small saucepan and warm over low heat.

▽ Add the sauce to the boulettes and let it reduce for a few more minutes.

▽ Serve the boulettes in the chamomile cream sauce alone or with with rice, lentils, quinoa, or mashed potatoes.

WITCH'S SECRET

You can use any kind of fish for this recipe. Even frozen fish. And for an even more succulent version, roll the boulettes in almond flour before cooking to give them extra crunch!

Fertility

SCALLOPS

 SERVES 4 30 MINUTES 45 MINUTES

There's a reason Botticelli chose a scallop shell for the goddess of love in *The Birth of Venus*. Scallops are believed to improve fertility. Even in the absence of a particular problem, hormonal balance is incredibly fragile, and strengthening this system benefits the whole body. So, we're going to mix scallops with other ingredients that support the reproductive system, in this case sweet potatoes, beets, and lentils. Lentils provide antioxidants, protect against thyroid and immune dysfunction, and are full of fiber, which rids the body of excess hormones. Scallops are bursting with B vitamins, especially vitamin B12, which is essential for ovulation and DNA synthesis. These little sea treasures are also rich in minerals, trace elements, omega-3s, and have one of the highest protein-to-gram ratio of any food out there.

FOR THE LENTIL AND BEET PUREE

- **7 OZ (200 G)** LENTILS
- **½** ONION, CHOPPED
- **1** THYME SPRIG
- **9 OZ (250 G)** COOKED BEETS
- **1** TBSP VIRGIN COCONUT OIL
- SALT AND PEPPER

FOR THE SWEET POTATO-GOAT CHEESE PUREE

- **2** SWEET POTATOES
- **1** THYME SPRIG
- SALT AND PEPPER
- **3½ OZ (100 G)** GOAT CHEESE

FOR THE SCALLOPS

- **2** TSP OLIVE OIL
- **4** SEA SCALLOPS
- **½** TSP LEMON JUICE
- SALT
- **4** THYME SPRIGS
- PEPPER

THE LENTIL AND BEET PUREE

▽ Cook the lentils in 1½ times their volume of water with the chopped onion and thyme leaves for around 20 minutes until the lentils are tender and the water is completely absorbed. Add the beets, coconut oil, salt, and pepper and cook for a few more minutes. With the help of an immersion blender, blend the mixture into a puree. Set aside.

THE SWEET POTATO-GOAT CHEESE PUREE

▽ Peel the sweet potatoes and cut them into small pieces. Cook them in boiling water in another pot with the thyme leaves, salt, and pepper for about 10 minutes until you can pierce them with a fork. Empty the water out of the pot and add the goat cheese. Blend into a puree. Set aside.

THE SCALLOPS

▽ Heat the olive oil in a small pan over very high heat. Just before the oil starts to burn (you don't want it to smoke, that means it's gotten too hot and can be bad for health), add the sea scallops. Cook them for about 1 minute a side.

▽ Do not move the scallops too much during cooking—this will ensure they are nicely browned. Turn them over and cook on the other side for about 1 minute. When they are almost cooked, add the lemon juice and a little salt. You can also add a thin slice of butter at the very end to enrich the flavor. Remove the scallops from the pan to stop them from cooking further.

▽ Reheat the purées and serve some of both on each plate. Add the scallops and 1 fresh thyme sprig and season with pepper.

Mackerel
FOR MELANCHOLY

 SERVES 4 · 20 MINUTES · 30 MINUTES

As a water element, fish possesses powers of immunity that protect the heart and brain but can also soothe a troubled mind. Mental suffering is as real as physical pain, even if we can't see it. This invisible suffering exists and needs to be treated, too. Witch's recipes can help. Of course, getting to the root cause of someone's depression can be complicated, but sometimes symptoms are aggravated by a nutritional imbalance. There is a connection, for example, between a lack of vitamin D and depression because this vitamin plays a crucial role in brain function. This is why the sun is associated with joy. Our body needs sun to synthesize vitamin D, and if we cannot get it from this star, we must extract the vitamin from our food. The greatest sources of vitamin D are fatty fish like mackerel, mushrooms like shiitake, and dairy products like cream, which contains more vitamin D than milk. Nuts like almonds contain tryptophan, the precursor to serotonin, known as the happiness hormone. Lastly, basil is an adaptogenic herb that helps with stress and mood balance.

- 1 ONION
- 3½ OZ (100 G) SHIITAKE MUSHROOMS
- 1 TBSP OLIVE OIL
- 5 TBSP (7 CL) WHITE WINE

- 6¾ FL OZ (20 CL) ORGANIC HEAVY CREAM
- 2 OZ (50 G) ALMOND FLOUR
- SALT AND PEPPER

- 5 BASIL LEAVES, MINCED
- 4 WHOLE MACKEREL (OR 1 LARGER FISH LIKE SEA BASS)

▽ Finely chop the onion and mushrooms and cook them in a pan with the oil for 10–15 minutes until they are caramelized and grilled.

▽ Pour in the wine and continue cooking over medium heat until the liquid is completely absorbed. Do the same with the cream. Then add the almond flour, a little salt and pepper, and the chopped basil.

▽ Preheat the oven to 400°F (200°C).

▽ Spoon the filling into each mackerel, place the fish in a baking dish, and bake for 10–15 minutes depending on their size.

WITCH'S SECRET

To make this spell even more powerful and original, add sliced red grapes to the filling. The many antioxidants found in grapes will maximize the power of vitamin D.

Illumination
PUMPKINS

 SERVES 4   15 MINUTES   25 MINUTES

These little stuffed pumpkins are hiding a spell to protect your skin, your largest organ and your body's shield from the outside world. Salmon is a superfood for your skin because of its high levels of omega-3 fatty acids, which hydrate the skin and make it glow. Putting oils on your skin isn't enough . . . to have truly radiant skin you also need to consume more oil. Don't forget that the fat found in fish, avocado, and nut oils has incredible healing powers. . . it's almost magical. Salmon is also packed with vitamin E, an antioxidant that protects the skin from free radicals and premature aging. The sweet potato and pumpkin provide beta-carotene (vitamin A) and vitamin C, which are essential for collagen formation and skin regeneration. It's not surprising that all of these foods are the same color, because they all contain strong doses of the same healing antioxidants. In nature, colors are symbols. You just have to know how to interpret them.

- 4 SMALL PUMPKINS, 3½ OZ (100 G) EACH
- ONE 3½ OZ (100 G) SALMON FILLET
- 1 SMALL SWEET POTATO (OR ½ LARGE SWEET POTATO)
- 3 SHALLOTS, MINCED
- 2 OZ (50 G) WALNUTS
- JUICE OF ¼ LEMON
- ½ AVOCADO, CHOPPED
- SALT AND PEPPER

▽ Preheat the oven to 400°F (200°C).

▽ Cut a circle around the stem of each pumpkin and remove the cap. Empty the inside using a spoon. Remove any fibers from the caps.

▽ Slice the salmon into small cubes and set aside. Peel and slice the sweet potato into small cubes the same size as the salmon and cook the sweet potatoes in boiling water with the minced shallots until the sweet potato is soft but not falling apart. Drain the water, then put the sweet potatoes in a bowl with the uncooked salmon.

▽ Chop the walnuts and dry roast them in a pan for a few minutes. Keep an eye on them because they burn very quickly.

▽ Add the toasted walnuts to the bowl with the salmon and sweet potato and mix everything together with the lemon juice, chopped avocado, and a little salt and pepper. Spoon the filling into each pumpkin, put the caps back on, and bake for 20–25 minutes.

▽ You can also prepare these ahead of time and cook them the day of.

WITCH'S SECRET

Keep the pumpkin seeds, wash, dry, and roast them in the oven with a little salt and oil at 350°F (180°C) for 10–15 minutes. Sprinkle these seeds filled with minerals and healthy fats on top of your salads (Rebirth Salad, p. 27), meats (Vitality Osso Buco, p. 102), and vegetable dishes.

WITCH'S SECRET

To give this dish even more caramelization, coat the onions in a mixture of equal parts balsamic vinegar, oil, and honey before cooking. You can also replace the salmon with tofu or another skin-supporting root vegetable like carrots for a vegan version.

Stuffed Onions with
ANTI-INFLAMMATORY MAGIC

  SERVES 4 · 15 MINUTES · 35 MINUTES

To fight inflammation effectively, all we have to do is call upon the magic of foods from the earth and ocean. Fish and nuts are rich in omega-3 fatty acids that neutralize inflammation in the body. Fatty fish like halibut and the oil from nuts and seeds can even help reduce pain and relieve symptoms of many diseases that are aggravated by inflammation. To fill this spell with benefits and maximize its power, we will invoke the magic of both water and earth. The fish (we are using halibut here, but cod, salmon, or mackerel work just as well) is cooked directly inside the onion. Onions possess significant anti-inflammatory properties and the almond flour, rich in vitamin E, also works against inflammation.

- **4** LARGE RED ONIONS
- **2** TSP OLIVE OIL
- **3½** OZ **(100 G)** HALIBUT

- **1** OZ **(30 G)** ALMOND FLOUR
- **3–4** CILANTRO, BASIL OR PARSLEY SPRIGS, CHOPPED

- JUICE OF ½ LEMON
- SALT AND PEPPER

▽ Preheat the oven to 350°F (180°C).

▽ Cut off the top of each onion. Remove the first layer of skin and hollow out the interior a little bit so you can stuff them.

▽ In a pan, sauté the onion centers you removed in the previous step with the oil over medium heat. Add a few spoonsful of water during cooking and scrape the bottom of the pan with a spatula to salvage the juices and help the onions caramelize. When the onions are very tender, put them in a bowl and blend into a puree using an immersion blender.

▽ Cut the halibut into small cubes and stir them into the onion puree along with the almond flour, chopped cilantro, lemon juice, salt, and pepper. Mix thoroughly.

▽ Spoon the filling into the onions and put the caps back on. Bake for 25 minutes and serve with rice or lentils.

Pine Needle
PROTECTIVE FISH

 SERVES 2 20 MINUTES ☐ 25 MINUTES

The number of healing plants is infinite, and their uses also seem limitless. Trees in particular have strong therapeutic properties and are full of minerals and vitamins. The pine is perhaps the most therapeutic of all trees. Its needles and bark are good sources of vitamins C and A, as well as several other vitamins and minerals. Pine is also anti-inflammatory, loaded with powerful antioxidants and endowed with antimicrobial properties. This is maybe why these trees, which do such a good job of relieving winter illnesses, prosper during that season. The vitamin E in almonds promotes good immune system function, and pine nuts are particularly rich in zinc, another immunity nutrient that is indispensable during the winter months. And mushrooms, as we know, are brimming with vitamin D, another great protector. Nature gives us what we need at just the right time. We just have to follow the rhythm of the seasons—the way witches do.

FOR THE ALMOND-CRUSTED FISH

- **2** FILLETS OF WHITEFISH (WHITING, SEA BREAM, SOLE, BASS)
- **2** TBSP OLIVE OIL
- SALT AND PEPPER
- **3** OZ **(80 G)** GROUND ALMONDS

- **2–3** PINE BRANCHES
- **¾** OZ **(20 G)** PINE NUTS

FOR THE MUSHROOM GRATIN

- **2** RED ONIONS
- **7** OZ **(200 G)** MUSHROOMS

- **1** TBSP OLIVE OIL
- SALT AND PEPPER
- **6¾** FL OZ **(20 CL)** ORGANIC CREAM (OR COCONUT/SOY CREAM)
- **¾** OZ **(20 G)** PINE NUTS

▽ Preheat the oven to 410°F (210°C).

THE ALMOND-CRUSTED FISH

▽ Brush the fish with olive oil and season with salt and pepper. Roll them in the ground almonds until they are thoroughly coated.

▽ Place the pine branches on a baking tray and arrange the breaded fish fillets on top of them. Sprinkle with pine nuts and set aside while you prepare the mushroom gratin. It will be more efficient and environmentally friendly to cook them at the same time.

THE MUSHROOM GRATIN

▽ Chop the onions and slice the mushrooms. Sauté them in a pan with the olive oil, salt, and pepper until they are tender and browned. Incorporate the cream and let the sauce reduce for a few minutes. Transfer the mixture to a small baking dish and cover with pine nuts.

▽ Cook the fish and the gratin in the oven at the same time for 15–20 minutes. The almond crust should be slightly browned, and the fish should be soft and moist on the inside.

WITCH'S SECRET

You should harvest more pine needles to prepare a Healing Pine Needle Syrup (p. 166) so you always have a winter treatment on hand. Make sure to only harvest branches from real pine trees, because there are many look-alike trees that may not be edible.

WITCH'S SECRET

Do you wish your octopus was a little more tender? Marinate in 2 parts water, 1 part white balsamic vinegar, and 1 part white wine with a pinch of salt. The vinegar and salt will not only bring flavor to the flesh, they will also tenderize it. When you are ready, remove the octopus from the marinade, dry it off, and cook it.

Octopus in Power
INK SAUCE

🍴 SERVES 4 　 ⏱ 15 MINUTES 　 ⬛ 35 MINUTES

We often associate the magic of fire with red meat—a food that is filled with iron. But this energy-giving mineral that strengthens our blood is present in even greater quantities in water elements. Shellfish like octopus, cuttlefish, squid, and oysters are excellent sources of iron as well as several other minerals, vitamins, and rare trace elements. Looking for a way to increase the power of octopus and cuttlefish in your recipes? Add some of their ink—this will infuse the dish with its protective properties. The ink from these water creatures is particularly rich in antioxidants and iron. This ingredient not only helps boost physical power, it also fights depression thanks to its high levels of tyrosine, an amino acid that regulates mood. And how could we not mention oysters in our quest for vigor? Their power can be intensified using the magic of exotic fruits and fire. Strength, joy, satiety, and culinary enjoyment. Water holds many therapeutic treasures, you just have to know how to cook them.

FOR THE SEAFOOD RICE

- 1 TBSP OLIVE OIL
- 12½ OZ (350 G) BLACK RICE
- 2 TBSP WHITE BALSAMIC VINEGAR
- SALT AND PEPPER
- 14 OZ (400 G) OCTOPUS BODY MEAT

- 5 OZ (150 G) OCTOPUS TENTACLES
- 7 TBSP (10 CL) TOMATO SAUCE
- 7 TBSP (10 CL) RED WINE
- 17½ OZ (500 G) MUSSELS
- ⅓ OZ (10 G) CUTTLEFISH INK

FOR THE PASSION FRUIT OYSTERS

- 4 OYSTERS
- ⅛ TSP FRESH GINGER, GRATED
- ½ PASSION FRUIT

THE SEAFOOD RICE

▽ Heat the oil in a large pan over high heat. Pour in the black rice and toast it for a few minutes. Cover the rice with an inch of water and add the white balsamic vinegar, salt, and pepper. Next add the octopus meat, tentacles, tomato sauce, and wine and reduce the heat. Cover the pan and let cook over low heat for 30 minutes. If the rice becomes too dry, add a little more wine and tomato sauce.

▽ Incorporate the mussels and the ink. Cover the pan and cook for around 3 minutes until the mussels open. Serve warm with extra pepper on the side.

THE PASSION FRUIT OYSTERS

▽ Preheat the oven to 375°F (190°C).

▽ Open the oysters and place a pinch of grated ginger and passion fruit on top each one. Bake for 2–3 minutes until lightly cooked.

Satiety Shrimp
WITH ENDIVE CREAM

 SERVES 6 10 MINUTES 20 MINUTES

The saddest meal—and also the one that most symbolizes dieting—might just be eating half a grapefruit in the morning to curb your appetite. It's true that grapefruit is packed with antioxidants and that it helps us feel full, but we can certainly make it more joyful and even more filling. Shrimp are rich in protein that preserves our muscles and helps the body process fat and are also very low in calories and unhealthy, saturated fat. Endives, which are also low in calories and packed with antioxidants, are caramelized in coconut cream in this recipe. Coconut cream is rich in a healthy form of saturated fat that increases good cholesterol and makes us feel full and helps the body better process fat. Watching your weight? No problem. But that's no reason to eat boring food or not enough. The secret to a balanced weight is preparing whole and healthy foods with plenty of nutrients in a delicious way.

- 3 GRAPEFRUITS
- 1 APPLE
- 2 ENDIVES
- ⅓ OZ (10 G) BUTTER
- SALT AND PEPPER
- 5 FL OZ (15 CL) COCONUT CREAM
- 5 OZ (150 G) RAW PEELED SHRIMP
- 1 AVOCADO
- JUICE OF ¼ LEMON
- LAMB'S LETTUCE
- HERBS, GRATED FRESH GINGER, OR CHILI PEPPER FLAKES FOR SERVING

▽ Cut the grapefruits in half and carefully scrape out the pulp. Set aside the two grapefruit halves for later.

▽ Remove the membrane around the grapefruit pulp. Dice the apple into very small pieces. Set aside.

▽ Chop the endives and cook them in a pan over medium heat with the butter, salt, and pepper until caramelized (around 10 minutes). Add the coconut cream and let the mixture reduce until the liquid is completely absorbed.

▽ Add the shrimp and cook them until pink (around 2 minutes—if you are using cooked shrimp, just let them heat up).

▽ Remove from the heat, add the grapefruit pulp and apple pieces, and mix well. Spoon this mixture into the grapefruit halves. Cut the avocado in half and use a melon baller (or a small measuring spoon) to form small balls. Place these on top of the stuffed grapefruits and sprinkle with a few drops of lemon juice to preserve their color.

▽ Serve warm or cold with a garnish of lamb's lettuce and a sprinkling of herbs, grated fresh ginger, or chili pepper flakes.

WITCH'S SECRET

Many other foods are also endowed with the power of satiety: pine nuts, sweet potatoes, eggs, dried figs, oats, apples, oranges, and chia seeds. You can even switch up this recipe by integrated some of these ingredients, like sweet potatoes instead of shrimp for a vegan version.

Wisdom
CRAB

  SERVES 4 20 MINUTES 20 MINUTES

All water foods support cognitive health, but crab is a superfood in this area thanks to its many trace elements like copper, vitamin B2, selenium, and omega-3s. Crab's healthy fat also protects the brain and nervous system and supports heart health and detox mechanisms. As a general rule, healing foods that protect the brain also protect the heart. This wisdom crab recipe shows us that when it comes to diet, the heart and mind are much more connected than we think.

- 7–9 OZ (200–250 G) POTATOES (PURPLE VITELOTTE VARIETY IF POSSIBLE)
- 2 ROSEMARY SPRIGS
- SALT (FOR THE POTATOES)
- 2 COOKED CRABS
- 2 SHALLOTS, MINCED
- JUICE OF ½ LEMON
- SALT AND PEPPER
- 2 OZ (50 G) GROUND ALMONDS

▽ Cook the potatoes in a pot of boiling water with half of the rosemary leaves and the salt for around 20 minutes. When you can easily pierce them with a knife, drain the water and transfer the potatoes to a cold-water bath for a few minutes. Then remove the skin.

▽ Preheat the oven to 350°F (180°C).

▽ Remove the crab flesh and set aside the shell for later. Mash the potatoes roughly with a spoon and mix in the crab, minced shallots, lemon juice, and the rest of the rosemary leaves (minced). Add a little extra salt and pepper if necessary.

▽ Spoon this mixture into the crab shells and cover with ground almonds to form a crust. Drizzle with oil to ensure extra crispiness. Bake for 20 minutes.

WITCH'S SECRET

If you want to cook live crabs yourself, here are a few tips: place them in the freezer for 30 minutes to numb them before cooking them in boiling water, legs facing down, for 12–15 minutes depending on the size.

Jubilation

FISH

🍽 SERVES 2   ⏱ 15 MINUTES   🔲 55 MINUTES

Here is another delicious and healing recipe infused with water magic. A fish that will make you *and* your taste buds jubilant. Fish is full of healthy fats that help balance mood with high levels of vitamin D, but did you know that fennel also has euphoric and even aphrodisiac properties? This plant is often overlooked as a healing ingredient, but it is full of antioxidants that help release endorphins, our joy hormones that improve mood and fight anxiety. Even lemon has calming powers. Who would have thought that one of the secrets to a joyful life could be found in such a familiar food? Witches, of course.

- 2 FENNEL BULBS
- 2 TBSP OLIVE OR GRAPESEED OIL
- JUICE AND ZEST OF 1 ORGANIC LEMON, DIVIDED

- 7 TBSP (10 CL) ORGANIC HEAVY CREAM
- 3½ TBSP (5 CL) WHITE WINE
- SALT AND PEPPER

- 17½–21 OZ (500–600 G) WHITEFISH LIKE COD

▽ Preheat the oven to 400°F (200°C).

▽ Cut the fennel into ¾-inch slices and cook them in a large pan with the oil for at least 15 minutes until translucent and lightly caramelized. Add half of the lemon juice and zest during cooking. If the fennel starts sticking to the pan, add a few spoonsful of water to deglaze.

▽ Transfer the fennel slices to a baking tray lined with parchment paper and bake for 20 minutes.

▽ In the fennel pan, add the cream, white wine, and the remaining lemon juice. Season with salt and pepper and reduce for a few minutes.

▽ Salt and pepper the fish on both sides. Take the fennel slices out of the oven and place the fillets of fish on top of them. Cover with the cream sauce.

▽ Bake the fish and fennel for around 15 minutes (more or less, depending on the thickness of the fillets) until the fish turns from translucent to white in color. Serve sprinkled with the rest of the lemon zest.

WITCH'S SECRET

Do you have leftover fennel or fish? Make a Detox Salmon Salad (p. 98). As the scientist (or witch) Antoine Lavoisier says, "Nothing is lost, nothing is created; everything is transformed." Always look for ways to give new life to food left over from your other recipes.

Asparagus Tagliatelle
FOR THE HEART

 SERVES 2   10 MINUTES   10 MINUTES

Why just cook the vegetables we love when we can transform them into something else? Transformation is part of the art of witchcraft. Did you know that asparagus can be turned into tagliatelle and cooked like pasta? Just like salmon, asparagus promotes the healthy function of several systems in our body, but its primary benefits go straight to our heart and circulatory system. The soluble fiber in asparagus helps clean the arteries of plaque and prevents the formation of blood clots, and the good fat in salmon supports the health of the heart itself. When we maximize the healing effects of certain foods, we can allow ourselves to indulge with something like cream: it may be high in calories and cholesterol, but it's also filled with calcium and other essential minerals. Pleasure is important for heart health, too!

- **1** BUNCH GREEN ASPARAGUS
- **7** OZ **(200 G)** SALMON
- **2** TSP OLIVE OIL
- **6¾** FL OZ **(20 CL)** ORGANIC CRÈME FRAÎCHE **(**OR SOUR CREAM OR COCONUT CREAM**)**
- JUICE OF ½ LEMON
- SALT AND PEPPER

▽ Trim off the hard end of each asparagus spear. Cut off the heads and set aside. Using a vegetable peeler, peel the asparagus stalks to form tagliatelle-like ribbons. To make this process easier, place the asparagus flat on your work surface while peeling rather than trying to peel them vertically.

▽ Cut the salmon into small cubes and place them in a pan with the olive oil. Add the asparagus heads and tagliatelle and cook for a few minutes.

▽ Incorporate the crème fraîche, lemon juice, salt, and pepper and let the sauce reduce by half over low heat. Serve warm or keep to eat cold the next day.

WITCH'S SECRET

Looking for a way to remove the tough part of an asparagus spear? No need for a knife, just bend each spear near the bottom and it will break by itself, naturally bending just above the tough part. For a vegan option, just replace the salmon with a heart-supporting vegetable like white beans.

Detox Salmon
SALAD

🌿 🍽️ SERVES 4 ⏱️ 15 MINUTES 🔲 10 MINUTES 🌿

The body is a detox machine in itself. There is no magical food or diet in existence capable of triggering a weeklong "cleanse"—we are in a permanent state of detox because this is the job our kidneys and liver are doing every day. There are, however, certain foods and plants that can support this detoxification process. All of the ingredients in this spell play a role. Fennel has a mild diuretic effect, which is important for a gentle detox. Unfortunately, marketed detox herbs can be so powerful that their diuretic effects can damage the fragile kidneys if taken in too large quantities. Beets, artichokes, onions, radishes, and lemon gently stimulate kidney and liver activity thanks to their significant levels of antioxidants. Salmon, like other fatty fish, is full of omega-3s essential for good liver function and its detox mechanisms. Want to optimize your body's detox abilities? Incorporate ingredients rich in antioxidants and omega-3s into your diet every day. With a little culinary magic, you'll be delighted by the flavors of this dish while your body silently incorporates its beneficial health effects.

FOR THE SALMON SALAD

- **14** OZ **(400** G) SALMON
- **2** TBSP OLIVE OIL
- JUICE OF **1** LEMON
- SALT AND PEPPER
- **2** FENNEL BULBS

- **1** RED ONION
- **3–4** SMALL COOKED BEETS
- **3½** OZ **(100** G) CANNED ARTICHOKE HEARTS
- A FEW HANDFULS OF ARUGULA
- **2** OZ **(50** G) RADISHES, SLICED
- A FEW DILL SPRIGS

FOR THE DILL YOGURT DRESSING

- **10½** OZ **(300** G) YOGURT
- **2** DILL SPRIGS, CHOPPED
- JUICE OF **¼** LEMON
- SALT AND PEPPER

THE SALMON SALAD

▽ Cook the salmon in a pan with the olive oil. During cooking, add the lemon juice, salt, and pepper. You can poke the fish with a fork to see if it's cooked on the inside. The center of the fillet should be slightly medium rare but not raw. Remove from pan and let the fish cool.

▽ Slice the fennel and onion as thinly as possible (use a mandoline if you have one). Cut the beets and artichoke hearts into cubes or halves.

▽ On a large plate, create a bed of arugula leaves then add the fennel, beets, artichokes, and radish rounds. Break the salmon into pieces with a fork and arrange the pieces on top of the salad.

THE DILL YOGURT DRESSING

▽ In a small bowl, mix together the yogurt, chopped dill, lemon juice, salt, and pepper until smooth.

▽ Pour the dressing over the salad and garnish with dill sprigs.

WITCH'S SECRET

Even if fatty fish are good for our health, they are also loaded with toxic heavy metals—the exact opposite of detox. But there is a food spell to protect us: add a small spoonful of chlorella (a unicellular form of green algae) to fish recipes (you can also consume it in pill form). This alga binds to the metals contained in fish and neutralizes them before they can be absorbed by our system.

FOREST STEW (SEE RECIPE ON P. 106)

Fire RECIPES

△

MEAT
LIFE FORCE RECIPES

The benefits of the water element come from fish and shellfish, and we receive the benefits of the air element in the form of poultry. Fruits and vegetables provide nutrients from the earth element. **Fire, the final element—our life force, embodied in the sun—comes to us in red meat and white meats like rabbit and pork.** Ideally, we would eat a primarily vegetarian diet, but for a healthy balance, especially for children, it's a good idea to eat a certain amount of meat. Our ancestors had a plant-based diet, but as a result of earth's changing cycles and climate, they were forced to incorporate meat little by little. According to some, it was this change in diet that may have accelerated the brain's development. This may also explain why humans tolerate the fat and cholesterol in meat better than chimpanzees and other primates. While consuming certain kinds of fat in high quantities can cause problems, red meat offers unrivaled benefits in terms of energy and nutrients like iron, protein, B vitamins, and other essential minerals. But evolution always follows earth's cycles. Meat today is subjected to too many treatments, and we are depleting our resources in an attempt to produce enough of it. There is not enough space on our planet to satisfy the global demand for meat. The solution? Moderation. And choosing more environmentally sustainable meats like rabbit and pork. Even though we need the fire element for a balanced diet, we shouldn't consume large amounts of it. For personal health and the health of the planet, each person should limit their weekly consumption of meat. Another way to eat environmentally friendly? Choose organic and local meat. Witches know how important it is to respect the elements, the cycles of nature, and animals.

Vitality

OSSO BUCO

 SERVES 4   🕐 20 MINUTES   ⬛ 1 HOUR 30 MINUTES

There's an easy way to amplify meat's power: cook it with its bones. Too often, we throw out meat and vegetable parts that are perfectly usable. Beef bones, for instance, have healing and immuno-stimulant properties because of the minerals they contain. We can extract these benefits from bones with potions (see Bone Broth on p. 159), but for an even tastier approach we can cook them in a vitality spell. This recipe invokes the powers of dried fruits because the level of iron in plums and apricots increases when they are dried. The complex carbohydrates in sweet potatoes provide long-term energy, and the strong presence of vitamin C in this recipe helps the body absorb iron from the fruit and meat. We are so lucky that the flavors of these vitality foods go so well together! Or perhaps it isn't a coincidence.

- **4** PIECES OSSO BUCO (VEAL SHANKS)
- **¾** OZ **(20** G) FLOUR (OR GLUTEN-FREE FLOUR)
- **2** TBSP OLIVE OIL, DIVIDED
- **3** GARLIC CLOVES, MINCED
- **2** SWEET POTATOES
- **5** SHALLOTS

- **5** SMALL ONIONS
- **5** PRUNES
- **5** DRIED APRICOTS
- **3½** OZ **(100** G) BUTTON, OYSTER, OR SHIITAKE MUSHROOMS
- **⅞** OUNCE **(25** G) BUTTER
- **3½** TBSP **(5** CL) TOMATO SAUCE

- **7** TBSP **(10** CL) RED WINE
- **1** TBSP BALSAMIC VINEGAR
- **¼** TSP GROUND CINNAMON
- **¼** TSP GRATED NUTMEG
- SALT AND PEPPER
- PUMPKIN SEEDS TO GARNISH (OPTIONAL)

△ Preheat the oven to 350°F (180°C). Coat each piece of meat in flour and place them in a Dutch oven or large oven-safe pan with half of the oil and minced garlic. Brown the meat on all sides for 1–2 minutes. Remove the meat from the stewpot and set aside.

△ Prepare the vegetables: peel the sweet potatoes and cut them into slices just under one inch thick. Peel the shallots and small onions. Chop the prunes and dried apricots into very small pieces. Slice any large mushrooms and keep the rest whole. Add all of these vegetables to the Dutch oven along with the butter and remaining oil and cook for around 20 minutes over medium heat.

△ Next add the tomato sauce, red wine, balsamic vinegar, cinnamon, nutmeg, salt, and pepper. Mix well and let the sauce infuse with the fruits and onions for a few minutes over low heat.

△ Return the meat to the Dutch oven, coat with the sauce, and cover your pan or stewpot. Bake for 60–90 minutes until the meat easily separates from the bone. If the sauce reduces too much during cooking, add a few spoonsful of wine.

△ Serve the osso buco by itself with a garnish of pumpkin seeds or with a side of lentils to potentiate its energetic powers even more.

WITCH'S SECRET

I suggest preparing this dish the night before. The meat will be even more tender and flavorful. Cook the osso buco in a pan with the fruit and onion sauce for 20 minutes before letting it cool. Store in the refrigerator for up to 2 days. The day you plan to serve it, cook at 350°F (180°C) for around 1 hour 30 minutes.

WITCH'S SECRET

Not sure what to do with a large veal chop? To avoid having too many leftovers, remove some of the meat from the bone to use in future recipes. Freeze the additional meat for Veal Boulettes with Healing Herbs (p. 112), for example, and make sure to keep the bones to make a broth (p. 159).

Autumn Fruit
VEAL CHOPS

 SERVES 4 🕐 10 MINUTES 📟 30 MINUTES

Autumn is a generous season. The earth gives us her fruits and seeds filled with the nutrients we need to survive the winter. Apples and grapes are particularly rich in antioxidants that reinforce all of the body's processes and defense mechanisms during difficult winters. This protective magic is amplified by the fire power of the veal, a lean protein filled with energy generated B vitamins and essential minerals. An easy way to practice therapeutic magic is to eat seasonally. Nature gives us everything we need at the right time. There's a reason we find seasonal ingredients so delightful!

- **2** VEAL OR LAMB CHOPS
- **⅓** OZ **(10** G) FLOUR (OR GLUTEN-FREE FLOUR)
- **3** APPLES

- **⅞** OUNCE **(25** G) BUTTER
- **1** TBSP NEUTRAL OIL (LIKE GRAPESEED OR SUNFLOWER)
- **4–5** THYME SPRIGS

- SALT AND PEPPER
- **3½** TBSP **(5** CL) WHITE WINE
- **7** OZ **(200** G) GRAPES (SEEDLESS)
- **3½** TBSP **(5** CL) RED WINE

△ Remove the chops from the refrigerator 10 minutes before cooking to bring them to room temperature. Coat them in flour on both sides; this will keep in the juices during cooking.

△ Peel the apples and cut them into eighths.

△ Heat the butter and oil in a pan over high heat with leaves from a few thyme sprigs, salt, and pepper. Grill the chops for 2 minutes on each side. Remove from the pan and set aside.

△ Reduce the heat and place the apples in the pan. Cook them until soft. When the apples start sticking to the pan, deglaze with the white wine. After the wine is absorbed, add the grapes and cook for another few minutes.

△ Return the chops to the pan and turn up the heat. Cook the meat for 4–6 minutes on each side, depending on thickness and your preference. Add the red wine and a little more salt and pepper during cooking.

△ Serve the meat with a garnish of fresh thyme.

Forest STEW

 SERVES 4–6   30 MINUTES 🔥 2 HOURS 30 MINUTES

If there's any place that brings magic to mind, it's the forest. This stew is full of its powers. Mushrooms provide a variety of minerals and vitamin D, root vegetables like turnips and carrots are loaded with vitamins C and A, onions with antioxidants, and walnuts with omega-3 fatty acids. And rabbit meat is a marvelous source of energy. This little animal is not only a very eco-friendly meat, it is also particularly rich in trace elements like selenium and phosphorous, iron, B vitamins, and omega-3s. It contains even more healthy fat than poultry and pork. Enjoy this lifesaving woodland spell!

- 17½–21 oz (500–600 G) RABBIT (LOIN OR LEGS)
- ⅓ oz (10 G) FLOUR (OR GLUTEN-FREE FLOUR)
- 2 TBSP OLIVE OIL
- ⅓ oz (10 G) BUTTER

- 4 BLACK CARROTS
- 5 TURNIPS
- 9 oz (250 G) MUSHROOMS
- 2 CELERY STALKS
- 8–10 PEARL ONIONS
- 3½–5 oz (100–150 G) CHESTNUTS, CRUSHED

- A FEW SPRIGS OF THYME
- SALT AND PEPPER
- 34 FL OZ (1 LITER) CHICKEN OR BEEF STOCK, DIVIDED
- 8½ FL OZ (25 CL) RED WINE

△ Flour the rabbit pieces and place them in a Dutch oven or oven-proof pot with the olive oil and butter. Brown on all sides for 1–2 minutes. Remove the meat from the pot and set aside.

△ Peel and slice the carrots into rounds and the turnips and mushrooms into quarters. Finely chop the celery stalks. Peel the onions and leave them whole.

△ Put all of these vegetables into the Dutch oven along with the crushed chestnuts, thyme, salt, and pepper, and let cook for 30 minutes, basting regularly with some of the chicken or beef stock.

△ Next add the rest of the stock, the wine, and the rabbit. Cover the stewpot and cook over low heat for 2 hours. Check periodically to make sure the mixture is not sticking too much to the bottom of the pot.

△ Serve this stew nice and hot with a side of rice or quinoa.

WITCH'S SECRET

To make the rabbit meat even more tender and bursting with flavor, let it marinate in wine with a few spoonsful of honey and balsamic vinegar the night before you cook it.

Mini Shepherd's Pies
FOR ANEMIA

 SERVES 4 **20 MINUTES** **30 MINUTES**

Did you know the French version of this classic dish was invented by a culinary witch? Antoine Parmentier, an eighteenth-century pharmacist and nutritionist, used to tout healthy foods like potatoes as a source of energy. This spell against anemia is inspired by his desire to share his knowledge of health. These mini shepherd's pies (or "*hachis parmentier*," as they are called in France) will boost your energy thanks to the unusual combination of spinach, lentils, and dried figs and apricots, all of which are high in iron, paired with the high concentrations of vitamins found in beef liver. The high level of vitamin C in these foods promotes the absorption of iron and digestive enzymes, which also help digest the protein in the meat. Antoine Parmentier would certainly be proud of the culinary progress witches have made today.

- 3½ OZ (100 G) LENTILS
- 2–3 HANDFULS OF SPINACH
- 6¾ FL OZ (20 CL) CASHEW CREAM
- SALT AND PEPPER
- 3½ OZ (100 G) DRIED APRICOTS (ABOUT 12)
- 7 TBSP (10 CL) RED WINE, DIVIDED
- 7 OZ (200 G) GROUND BEEF
- ¾ OZ (20 G) BEEF LIVER
- ⅓ OZ (10 G) BUTTER
- 2 THYME SPRIGS
- 3½ OZ (100 G) DRIED FIGS (ABOUT 5)
- 7 OZ (200 G) MUSHROOMS
- 1 TBSP SUNFLOWER OR OLIVE OIL

For this recipe, we will build the mini shepherd's pies in several layers. It is easier to use mousse molds with a pusher or mini cake molds with a detachable base, but you can also make them by hand, one layer at a time.

THE FIRST LAYER: LENTILS AND SPINACH
△ Cook the lentils in a pot of boiling water for around 20 minutes. Drain the water and add the spinach leaves, cashew cream, salt, and pepper. Continue cooking until the cream reduces by half. Set aside.

THE SECOND LAYER: APRICOTS
△ Finely dice the dried apricots and cook them in a pan with half of the wine for a few minutes until the wine is absorbed. Set aside.

THE THIRD LAYER: GROUND BEEF AND LIVER
△ Sauté the ground beef and liver in a pan with the butter, thyme leaves, salt, and pepper. Stir well and set aside.

THE FOURTH LAYER: FIGS
△ Finely chop the dried figs into small pieces and cook them in a pan with the rest of the wine until the liquid is absorbed. Set aside.

THE FIFTH LAYER: MUSHROOMS
△ Slice the mushrooms (leave the smaller ones whole) and cook them in a pan with the sunflower oil until they are browned and reduced in size. Lightly salt.

△ Assemble the shepherd's pie layer by layer and finish with the mushrooms.

WITCH'S SECRET

For a more rustic, family-style version, you can prepare this spell in one large baking dish rather than individual portions. Prepare the layers as described above and then cook at 350°F (180°C) for 20 minutes after assembling all of the layers to further infuse the flavors.

Detox Stuffed
CABBAGE

 SERVES 4–6 25 MINUTES 🔲 50 MINUTES

These little stuffed cabbages are inhabited by protective magic. They are cooked with onions, tomato sauce, and cranberries, all of which are rich in antioxidants. The meat is a tremendous source of energy and protein and the cabbage caramelized in balsamic vinegar supports detox mechanisms and digestive and heart health because of its high fiber content. The antioxidant-rich cranberries offer this dish a fruity flavor and are good for the kidneys and liver detox *support*. The walnuts contain healthy fat that is essential for proper brain and liver function. Detox spells don't have to be limited to salads and green juices. Warm, comforting, and delicious dishes can also help detoxify the body.

- 2 ONIONS
- 2 TBSP OLIVE OIL
- SALT AND PEPPER
- 1 HEAD GREEN CABBAGE
- 17½ OZ (500 G) GROUND BEEF

- A FEW THYME, ROSEMARY, AND OREGANO SPRIGS, FINELY MINCED, DIVIDED
- 1½ OZ (40 G) DRIED CRANBERRIES
- 2 OZ (50 G) WALNUTS, CHOPPED

- 14 OZ (400 G) TOMATO SAUCE
- 3½ OZ (100 G) TOMATO PASTE
- 4 TSP (2 CL) RED WINE
- 2 TBSP (3 CL) OLIVE OIL
- 2 TBSP (3 CL) BALSAMIC VINEGAR

△ Chop the onions and sauté in a pan for 5 minutes with the olive oil, salt, and pepper.

△ Separate the cabbage leaves and boil 4–6 of the most beautiful leaves in a pot for 20 minutes. Remove the leaves from the water and dry. Use a knife to remove one inch of the tough stem in the center of each leaf to make it easier to wrap around the stuffing.

△ Preheat the oven to 400°F (200°C).

△ In a bowl, mix together the beef, caramelized onions, a few of the sprigs of fresh herbs, cranberries, chopped walnuts, and a pinch of salt and pepper. Place a few spoonsful of filling on each cabbage leaf. Fold up each one like a little purse and lay them on a plate, seam-face down to keep them from unraveling, while you prepare the sauce.

△ Pour the tomato sauce, tomato paste, red wine, and the rest of the fresh herbs into a baking dish. Stir together. Gently transfer the stuffed cabbage purses into the tomato sauce. Drizzle with olive oil and balsamic vinegar.

△ Bake for 30 minutes until the cabbage is caramelized and lightly grilled.

△ Serve the stuffed cabbage purses by themselves or with a side of pasta or whole grains.

WITCH'S SECRET

How do you know when a roast is cooked, but not overdone? The most sensible method is to use a meat thermometer—the temperature at the center should be 160°F (70°C). The meat should be slightly browned on the surface and moist on the inside. For a more skilled approach, press the meat with your finger, it should give in slightly while still feeling firm.

Creation Honey
PORK ROAST

🍽 SERVES 4–6   ⏱ 30 MINUTES + 20 MINUTES (MARINADE)   🔲 1 HOUR

The spectrum of nutrients we need to create life is wide-ranging and involves supporting several of the body's mechanisms at once. It is not simply a question of reproduction, but the balancing of the entire hormonal system. To promote fertility, the best diet is one that is unprocessed and rich in protein, fruits, and vegetables. Would you be surprised if I told you that pork is a fertility superfood? It is loaded with protein, and this fire element is also filled with hormone-balancing B vitamins, including vitamin B6, one of the most important nutrients for conception. The significant levels of minerals like selenium also help increase fertility. And to amplify these benefits, we marinate the pork in honey, which is full of amino acids and minerals. We then cook it over a bed of white beans, an excellent source of fiber that helps clean out the body and prevent hormonal disturbances.

FOR THE MARINADE

- 2¼ OZ (60 G) HONEY
- ¾ OZ (20 G) MUSTARD
- 2 TBSP WINE
- A FEW THYME SPRIGS
- 1 TBSP OLIVE OIL
- SALT AND PEPPER

FOR THE ROAST

- 35 OZ (1 KG) PORK ROAST
- 7 OZ (200 G) TURNIPS OR BABY TURNIPS
- 2 ONIONS
- 2 TBSP OLIVE OIL
- 17½ OZ (500 G) COOKED WHITE BEANS
- SALT AND PEPPER
- 4–5 THYME SPRIGS
- SEEDS OF ½ POMEGRANATE

△ Mix together all of the marinade ingredients in a bowl. Lightly score the top of the roast with a knife so the marinade can penetrate the meat. Place it in a deep bowl, cover with the marinade, and let rest for 20 minutes (or even overnight).

△ Preheat the oven to 350°F (180°C).

△ Peel the turnips and slice them in quarters. Chop the onions and sauté them for 10 minutes with the olive oil and beans in an oven-safe pot with a little salt and pepper and leaves from 2–3 thyme sprigs.

△ Place the roast on top of the beans and add the turnips. Cover the pot and bake for about 1 hour.

△ Remove the roast from the oven and add the pomegranate seeds, which will lend the dish a fruity touch and extra boost of creation magic.

△ Let the roast rest for 15 minutes before slicing so the meat can reabsorb its juices.

Veal Boulettes
WITH HEALING HERBS

 SERVES 4 20 MINUTES ▣ 25 MINUTES

It is during moments of physical weakness that joy is most essential, for both the body and mind. That is where the pleasure and comfort of food comes in. These veal boulettes with healing herbs, served with zucchini tagliatelle, remind us of meals our grandmothers made when we were children. But these boulettes are also filled with the magic of herbs and their antiviral, antibacterial, and immunostimulant properties. The zucchini tagliatelle in an antioxidant-rich tomato sauce makes this recipe even healthier and maximizes its healing power. Pleasure reigns supreme for food-loving witches!

FOR THE VEAL BOULETTES

- **17½ OZ (500 G)** GROUND VEAL (OR LAMB)
- **2 OZ (50 G)** BREAD CRUMBS (OR GLUTEN-FREE BREAD CRUMBS)
- **1** EGG
- A FEW SPRIGS OF HEALING HERBS (ROSEMARY, THYME, BASIL, TARRAGON), MINCED
- SALT AND PEPPER
- **1** TBSP OLIVE OIL

FOR THE ZUCCHINI TAGLIATELLE

- **6–8** ZUCCHINI
- **2** ONIONS
- **2** GARLIC CLOVES, MINCED
- **2** TBSP OLIVE OIL
- **6¾** FL OZ **(20 CL)** TOMATO SAUCE
- **3** ROSEMARY SPRIGS, MINCED
- SALT AND PEPPER
- A FEW BASIL LEAVES TO GARNISH (OPTIONAL)
- GRATED CHEESE (OPTIONAL)

THE VEAL BOULETTES

△ If the meat is not already ground, cut it into small pieces and grind in a mixer. Add the bread crumbs, egg, minced herbs, salt, and pepper and mix thoroughly. Form small balls the size of apricots and set them aside while you prepare the zucchini tagliatelle and sauce.

THE ZUCCHINI TAGLIATELLE

△ Peel the zucchini and use a spiralizer, mandoline, or cheese grater to make the tagliatelle. Peel the onions and cut them in half, then slice them as finely as the zucchini.

△ Heat the olive oil in a large pan and add the zucchini, onions, and minced garlic. Cook for at least 10 minutes. Add the tomato sauce, rosemary leaves, salt, and pepper. Mix thoroughly and set aside.

△ Heat olive oil in a separate pan over medium heat and add the boulettes along with a little salt and pepper. Cook them for around 10 minutes until browned on all sides.

△ Transfer the boulettes to the pan with the zucchini and cook everything together for 5 more minutes, making sure the boulettes are covered in sauce.

△ If you like, you can serve these boulettes with fresh, minced basil and grated cheese.

WITCH'S SECRET

Don't pack your boulettes together too tightly or they will turn rubbery after cooking. Also, put them in the refrigerator before cooking them—this will keep the fat from melting the moment they hit the pan and help keep them intact. Make sure that the boulette mixture is wet enough; if it is too dry, add 1 egg. If it is too wet, add more bread crumbs. Looking for an easier way to cook them? Bake them in the oven for 10–12 minutes at 350°/400°F (180°/200°C).

Drunken Cider Pork
FOR LUMINOUS SKIN

🍴 SERVES 4   ⏱ 15 MINUTES + 1 HOUR (MARINADE)   🔲 30 MINUTES

Pork is often considered a fatty meat, and this is true to an extent. Certain parts of this fire animal contain too much saturated fat, which increases cholesterol, **but there are also leaner parts that contain as much healthy fat and as many nutrients as poultry.** These lean cuts have even fewer calories than chicken. An unexpected benefit found in pork is that it supports the skin's health and beauty; its richness in minerals and vitamin B3 (niacin) combats acne and inflammation. To amplify these benefits, we are serving it with earth foods like sweet potatoes, pumpkin, and hard apple cider. They are loaded with vitamin C and beta-carotene (vitamin A), which play a major role in collagen production.

- **4** BONELESS PORK CHOPS
- **10** FL OZ (**30** CL) HARD CIDER
- **4–5** THYME SPRIGS

- SALT AND PEPPER
- **⅞** OUNCE (**25** G) BUTTER
- **2** TBSP OLIVE OIL

- **3** SMALL SWEET POTATOES
- **1** RED KURI SQUASH

△ Marinate the pork chops in the hard cider with the thyme sprigs, salt, and pepper for 1 hour.

△ Preheat the oven to 350°F (180°C). Drain the meat and set the marinade aside for later. Heat the butter and olive oil in a pan over high heat. When the oil becomes very hot, add the pork and brown each side for around 2 minutes. Then remove it from the pan.

△ Peel and slice the sweet potatoes. Peel the squash and then cut it in half and then into slices.

△ Arrange the vegetables on a baking tray lined with parchment paper. Cover them with half of the marinade, season with salt and pepper, and bake for around 15 minutes until the vegetables are tender and slightly browned.

△ Remove the vegetables from the oven and add the pork chops. Cover the meat with the rest of the marinade and season with salt and pepper. Bake for around 12 more minutes until the pork is cooked through.

WITCH'S SECRET

For pork with even more magic for your skin, marinate it in hard cider and a few spoonsful of apple cider vinegar the entire night before you cook it.

Beef Stuffed Peppers
FOR PROTECTION

 SERVES 4   20 MINUTES   40 MINUTES

There's an easy way to get your dose of antioxidants while eating red meat: cook it in a pepper with other magical ingredients! Peppers offer one of the highest sources of vitamin C and they also provide many other protective antioxidants. Mushrooms support immunity thanks to their high levels of vitamin D and fight premature skin aging with their antioxidants. Parsley is also particularly high in vitamin C, which promotes immunity and good skin health. Meat is an essential part of a balanced diet, and there is always a way to give it even greater healing powers and make it even more delicious by preparing it with foods from the earth.

- **1** ONION
- **7** OZ **(200 G)** MUSHROOMS
- **1** TBSP OLIVE OIL
- SALT AND PEPPER
- **3½** TBSP **(5 CL)** RED WINE
- **14** OZ **(400 G)** GROUND BEEF
- A FEW PARSLEY SPRIGS, CHOPPED
- **4** BELL PEPPERS

△ Preheat the oven to 400°F (200°C).

△ Chop the onion and slice the mushrooms. Cook them in a pan with olive oil for around 10 minutes until they are tender and browned. Season with salt and pepper and add the red wine

△ Remove from the heat, incorporate the ground beef and chopped parsley, and mix thoroughly.

△ Cut off the top of each pepper and scoop out the seeds and white membranes on the inside. Divide the filling between the peppers. Put the tops back on and bake the stuffed peppers for 30 minutes.

△ Serve warm, decorated with fresh herbs.

WITCH'S SECRET

This recipe works just as well with chicken or turkey. You can even make a filling using salmon, whitefish, or shrimp to enjoy the benefits of the water element, or replace the meat with lentils or peas for a vegan version.

Aphrodisiac
STEAK

 SERVES 2   10 MINUTES   10 MINUTES

> Red meat is already a bearer of vitality, but there are ways to amplify the benefits of this fire element. **Witches, for example, combine it with the power of beets. This bloodred root is the ultimate love food.** It increases blood circulation and energy production thanks to its elevated levels of nitric oxide and stimulates the entire body, in particular the libido. Pistachios and saffron also have aphrodisiac virtues. And the wine? Everyone already knows about its powers of emancipation. . . Using natural elements to strengthen the body, bring emotions to the surface, and provide pleasure is the most intimate kind of witch's magic.

FOR THE BEET CARPACCIO

- 10½ oz (300 g) cooked beets
- 2 oz (50 g) grapes
- 1 oz (30 g) pistachios, crushed
- 1 tsp olive oil
- 2 tsp white balsamic vinegar
- salt and pepper

FOR THE APHRODISIAC SAUCE

- 1 tbsp beet juice
- 3½ tbsp (5 cl) red wine
- 1 tbsp balsamic vinegar
- pinch of saffron

FOR THE STEAK

- 2 beef tenderloin steaks or tournedos
- 2¾–3½ tbsp (4–5 cl) grapeseed oil, divided
- salt and pepper
- ⅞ ounce (25 g) butter
- pinch of saffron

△ Remove the meat from the refrigerator 10 minutes before cooking to bring it to room temperature.

THE BEET CARPACCIO

△ Cut the beets into very thin, almost translucent slices and arrange them on plates to form rosettes. Slice the grapes in the same way and arrange them on top of the beets. Sprinkle with crushed pistachios. In a small bowl, mix together the olive oil, vinegar, and a pinch of salt and pepper and pour the sauce over the carpaccio.

THE APHRODISIAC SAUCE

△ In a small bowl, mix together the beet juice, wine, balsamic vinegar, and saffron. Set aside.

THE STEAK

△ Drizzle the steaks with a bit of the grapeseed oil and season generously with salt and pepper.

△ Heat the rest of the grapeseed oil (which has a very high smoke point) in a pan over high heat. When the oil starts to crackle, add the steaks. Don't move them! After 1 minute, add the butter and a pinch of saffron. Tilt the pan and use a spoon to baste the steaks with the juices. Cook for 4–6 minutes on each side.

△ After turning over the steaks, pour 1 spoonful of the aphrodisiac sauce into the pan. When the steaks are cooked to your liking (undercooked is always better than overcooked!), remove them from the pan and let them rest for at least 5 minutes so the meat can reabsorb the juices.

△ In the meantime, turn up the heat and pour the rest of the aphrodisiac sauce into the empty pan. Whisk constantly until it is reduced by half. It should be thick and a little caramelized.

△ Serve the steaks coated in the aphrodisiac sauce beside the beet carpaccio and wait to see what happens.

WITCH'S SECRET

Marinate the meat in beet juice, red wine, and balsamic vinegar overnight. Then cook it as described in this spell. The steak will be even more tender, and the aphrodisiac magic will be amplified.

WITCH'S SECRET

While it's best to use fresh produce for this recipe, frozen berries will also do the trick. They may even have more nutrients than the fresh fruits sold at the supermarket. Fresh berries are often harvested too early and ripen on store shelves and therefore contain fewer nutrients than fruits harvested at perfect ripeness before being frozen.

Jumping for
JOY VEAL

  SERVES 4 10 MINUTES 30 MINUTES

If you need an endorphin boost, there's a way to get it that is more enjoyable than jogging and more reasonable than eating chocolate all day long! The secret lies in berries, which are loaded with antioxidants that support the production of serotonin and dopamine, hormones linked to mood and pleasure (they are also involved in digestion and sleep). Veal is also a joy food because it is rich in tryptophan, an amino acid that contributes to serotonin production and cannot be produced by the body. The joyful ingredients in this spell work together to maximize their benefits for our mood, immunity, and energy.

- 2 TBSP SUNFLOWER OR OLIVE OIL
- 4 ROSEMARY SPRIGS, MINCED
- 23 OZ (650 G) VEAL MEDALLIONS

- 6 PEARL ONIONS OR 1 LARGE ONION
- 10½ OZ (300 G) BERRIES
- JUICE OF 2 CLEMENTINES

- 1½ OZ (40 G) HONEY
- SALT AND PEPPER
- 5–6¾ FL OZ (15–20 CL) RED WINE

△ Heat the oil and rosemary leaves in a large pan over high heat. Add the veal medallions and brown them on each side for 1–2 minutes. Remove them from the pan and set aside.

△ Chop the onions and add them to the pan. Sauté for 10 minutes, then add the berries, clementine juice, honey, salt, and pepper. Cook for 15–20 minutes until the berries and onions are caramelized and the liquid is absorbed. Pour in half the wine and continue cooking until it is absorbed.

△ Add the rest of the wine. Return the veal medallions to the pan and cook for another 5–6 minutes on each side.

△ Serve the medallions sprinkled with fresh, minced rosemary.

MATCHA ENERGY BALLS (SEE RECIPE ON P. 137)

Sweet
SPELLS

For any witch who loves cooking, pleasure is always first in her mind. And sweet pleasures are part of a balanced diet. There is a way to transform certain healthy ingredients without using sugar, butter, or even cream. Of course, the benefits of these last three ingredients cannot be replaced in all recipes. I would never suggest a radical approach.

My motto when it comes to sweets? Moderation. And moderation in moderation. My one piece of advice when it comes to my sweet spells? Don't hold back, because all of the ingredients used in these recipes are loaded with restorative benefits and delicious flavors. Why limit our consumption of desserts and pastries when we can simply transform them so that they do more good for us? It ought to be acknowledged that enjoyment is just as important as taking care of one's health.

Candle Illusion
CAKES

  SERVES 4 🕐 40 MINUTES 🔲 15 MINUTES

Transformation, sublimation, and illusion are all part of culinary magic, and illusion in particular can make cooking fun, especially when it comes to sweet spells. These illusion candles are hiding vegetables and other products of the earth that are rich in healing benefits. Carrots, a source of vitamins A and C, maintain good collagen balance, eye health, and immune system function. Goat milk yogurt is rich in enzymes and probiotics and plays a role in healthy digestion, gut microbiota, and immune function, and coconut oil and almonds provide healthy fats that stimulate detox and defense mechanisms. Even the spices used here are full of anti-inflammatory and immunostimulant powers. The real magic of this healthy and rich dessert? You can eat as much of it as you want! They are made mostly with vegetables, after all...

WET INGREDIENTS

- **5** CARROTS
- **4½** OZ **(125** G) GOAT MILK YOGURT
- **2** EGGS
- **7** OZ **(200** G) HONEY
- **2** TBSP VIRGIN COCONUT OIL

DRY INGREDIENTS

- **3½** OZ **(100** G) FLOUR (OR GLUTEN-FREE FLOUR)
- **2** OZ **(50** G) ALMOND FLOUR
- **2** TSP BAKING SODA
- **1** TSP BAKING POWDER
- **1** TSP CINNAMON
- **¼** TSP GROUND GINGER
- **¼** TSP GROUND NUTMEG
- **½** TSP NATURAL VANILLA POWDER
- PINCH OF VIRGIN SALT

FOR THE GANACHE

- **25** OUNCES **(700** G) CREAM CHEESE (ROOM TEMPERATURE)
- **2** OZ **(50** G) AGAVE SYRUP
- **2** OZ **(50** G) MAPLE SYRUP
- **¼** TSP GROUND CINNAMON
- PINCH OF NATURAL VANILLA POWDER

☆ Preheat the oven to 350°F (180°C).

☆ Grate the carrots and mix them with the other wet ingredients. Blend into a puree.

☆ Add all of the dry ingredients to a separate bowl and stir together. Then stir them into the wet ingredients until your mixture has an even texture.

☆ Pour the batter into small molds (or one large cake mold for a single cake rather than individual portions) greased beforehand. Bake for 12–15 minutes for small cakes and 30–35 minutes for a large one. Once out of the oven, set them aside to cool.

THE SPICED GANACHE

☆ Mix all of the ingredients together in a bowl until you have a creamy texture.

☆ Slice the cakes horizontally to make layers, then use the ganache to frost between the layers and then frost the entire outside of the cake. Stick a small candle in the center of the cakes and cover the exposed part with icing so that only the wick is showing. To imitate dripping candle wax, mix the remaining ganache with a little bit of water, 1 teaspoon at a time, so it becomes a liquid just thin enough to drip. Pour the icing into a piping bag (you can also use a plastic bag or a small spoon) and decorate the cake with drips of "wax." Serve the cakes with the candles lit!

WITCH'S SECRET

For a lactose-free cake frosting, see Anti-Inflammatory Lemon Cake recipe (p. 130).

Marzipan Baked APPLES

SERVES 4 · 10 MINUTES · 20 MINUTES

What could be better than a dessert that isn't bad for our health? The magic of sweet spells allows us to use lower quantities of processed sugar and unhealthy fats while still being able to satisfy our sweet tooth. You will be surprised by the explosion of flavors—almonds caramelized in honey, walnuts, and fresh figs—hidden inside these apples. The high levels of minerals and antioxidants, vitamin C to fortify the skin and immune system, healthy fats that purify and help the body defend itself, iron for strength, and fiber to facilitate digestion make this the perfect snack for any time of day.

- 4–5 APPLES
- 2 FIGS
- 2 OZ (50 G) WALNUTS OR PISTACHIOS
- 2¼ OZ (60 G) ALMOND PASTE
- 2 OZ (50 G) GROUND ALMONDS
- 2 OZ (50 G) CEREAL GRAINS
- ⅓ OZ (10 G) HONEY

☆ Preheat the oven to 350°F (180°C).

☆ Cut off the top of each apple and use a spoon or knife to hollow out the center to make some room for the filling.

☆ Roughly chop the figs and walnuts. Melt the almond paste in the microwave oven. Mix the melted almond paste with the figs, walnuts, ground almonds, cereal, and honey. Spoon this filling into the apples and bake for 15 minutes.

☆ Eat these treats warm for breakfast, a snack, or even dessert.

WITCH'S SECRET

To make this spell even richer in iron, use dried figs and apricots! Iron levels are higher in dried fruits.

Moon Macarons
FOR DREAMING

 MAKES APPROXIMATELY 10 MACARONS    10 MINUTES   6 MINUTES

These macarons are meant to be eaten right after the moon rises. **They are filled with the magic of sleep and eating one of these mini moons will bring you deeper into your dreams.** While matcha tea provides energy and boosts concentration, it also increases the production of brain waves emitted during meditation and dreaming, which helps induce a deeper, more relaxing sleep. The almonds used as the base of these magical cookies help to improve sleep quality, as they are a source of the sleep-regulating hormone melatonin and have high magnesium levels, which also help relax muscles and treat sleep-related issues. These moons are also prepared with lavender-infused honey to help calm the nervous system and induce calm. Eat as many of these macarons as you like, and you will benefit from their many nutrients and enjoy a magical night in the hours that follow . . .

- 5 oz **(150 g)** ALMOND FLOUR
- 3 EGG WHITES
- 1 EGG YOLK
- 3½ TBSP **(5 CL)** LAVENDER SYRUP FOR TRANQUILITY **(P. 128)**
- ½ TSP COCONUT CREAM
- ⅓ oz **(10 G)** MATCHA POWDER

☆ Preheat the oven to 350°F (180°C).

☆ Mix all of the ingredients together in a bowl. Make sure your hands are damp, so the batter doesn't stick to them, then form small crescent moons and place them on a sheet of parchment paper.

☆ Bake the moon macarons for 6 minutes. They should be slightly crunchy on the outside and soft on the inside.

WITCH'S SECRET

To decorate your caramelized lavender macarons, boil lavender flowers in a saucepan with 2 parts water to 1 part honey for 30 minutes. Remove the flowers and dry them overnight. Sprinkle them on top of the moon macarons before baking.

Lavender Syrup
FOR TRANQUILITY

🌿 ▭ MAKES 1 JAR 🕐 3 HOURS TO 2 WEEKS 🌿

All witches must have a tranquility potion in their magic tool kit. I personally prefer making them in the form of a sweet spell. Everything goes down better with a little sugar. And a honey syrup infused with the magic of calming flowers is exactly what we need during periods of stress. Not to mention it's good for your health. You can also add this syrup to herbal teas, cakes, and even coffee to balance the effects of caffeine. The essential oils of this aromatic flower relax the nervous system and help stabilize mood. Some say lavender is more effective than pharmaceutical anti-anxiety medications. Between a pill and a homemade syrup infused with magical flowers, the witch will always try a recipe first.

- ⅙ oz **(5 g)** DRIED LAVENDER
- 9 oz **(250 g)** ORGANIC HONEY

☆ If you have fresh lavender, bake the flowers at 195°F (90°C) for 15 minutes. They must be completely dry to avoid introducing bacteria into the honey (and it will make your home smell incredible!).

☆ Remove the small flowers from their stems and place them in a glass jar with the honey.

☆ Infuse the honey with the lavender by placing the glass jar in a pot of gently boiling water (that comes ¾ up the side of the jar) over low heat for 3 hours. For a more powerful, slow-extraction version that invokes the power of the fire element, leave the jar of honey and flowers in the sun for 2 weeks. Strain honey through fine mesh filter to remove lavender flowers.

WITCH'S SECRET

Infuse the honey with ⅙ oz (5 g) of dried chamomile flowers in addition to the lavender for an even more deeply calming syrup. So calming, in fact, that it will help put you to sleep.

Levitating
ROSE

🌿 | ⊙ | SERVES 4–6   🕐 10 MINUTES + 4 HOURS OF RESTING 🌿

Levitation isn't limited to the magical world of Harry Potter. With a few cooking tricks, we can make roses levitate in a Japanese-inspired raindrop cake made with lychee juice. You can also make the cake disappear! In order to do this, just taste it—I guarantee you it will quickly vanish. You will be surprised by this dessert's light, fruity, and floral flavor. But the true magic of this sweet spell lies in the healing properties of roses. Like lychees, these edible flowers are rich in antioxidants and antibacterial properties. They can even fortify the immune system and fight anxiety, inflammation, and stress.

- **17** FL OZ **(50** CL) OF COLD WATER
- **17** FL OZ **(50** CL) LYCHEE JUICE
- **⅓** OZ **(10** G) HONEY
- **⅛** TSP ROSEWATER
- **1** TSP AGAR POWDER

- A FEW ROSES
- **7** OZ **(200** G) RASPBERRIES FOR DECORATION
- **7** OZ **(200** G) LYCHEES FOR DECORATION

☆ Pour 17 fl oz (50 cl) of cold water and the lychee juice into a pot. Add the honey and rosewater and stir. Then add the agar powder, whisking vigorously. Let the mixture infuse for 5 minutes.

☆ Cook over medium heat until the potion starts to boil. Remove from heat.

☆ Pour the potion into a stainless steel or glass bowl and add the whole roses or rose petals. Refrigerate the cake overnight so it can set.

☆ Decorate with fresh raspberries and lychees before serving.

WITCH'S SECRET

If you don't have rosewater, you can make it at home. Instead of using regular water for this recipe, you can boil the water with a handful of (scented and organic!) rose petals until the petals lose their color. Filter the water and let it cool before using as described in this recipe.

Anti-Inflammatory
LEMON CAKE

 SERVES 4–6 20 MINUTES | 30 MINUTES

Allergies and food intolerances are more and more common (and perhaps a little bit in fashion in some cases). Sometimes it's simply a case of diagnostic error, and the real problem might be linked to an intolerance of processed foods. Other times it can be life-threatening. An allergic reaction, whether mild or severe, is essentially an inflammatory reaction. Whatever the spectrum of intolerance, our guts and immune systems need a break. First, we need to be able to isolate the so-called "irritant" such as lactose, gluten, eggs, nuts, or processed sugar. Luckily, you don't have to deprive yourself of good food to maintain your health. This lemon cake is fluffy, flavorful, and light, and is also gluten-free, lactose-free, nut-free, egg-free, and contains no processed sugar. And all the ingredients possess powerful anti-inflammatory properties that help calm the body's allergy system. For this recipe, the expression "less is more" is perfectly appropriate.

FOR THE CAKE

- **4** FL OZ **(12** CL**)** AQUAFABA, LEFTOVER CHICKPEA WATER **(**THE EQUIVALENT OF **3** EGGS**)**
- **7** OZ **(200** G**)** AGAVE SYRUP
- JUICE OF **1** ORGANIC LEMON
- ZEST OF **2** ORGANIC LEMONS

- **7** TBSP **(10** CL**)** COCONUT CREAM
- **3½** TBSP **(5** CL**)** COCONUT OR SUNFLOWER OIL
- **7** OZ **(200** G**)** BUCKWHEAT FLOUR
- **½** TSP BAKING SODA
- PINCH OF VANILLA POWDER
- PINCH OF SALT
- OIL FOR THE MOLD

FOR THE COCONUT GLAZE

- **7** TBSP **(10** CL**)** COCONUT CREAM
- **2¼** OZ **(60** G**)** GRANULATED SUGAR
- PINCH OF VANILLA POWDER

THE CAKE

☆ Preheat the oven to 350°F (180°C).

☆ Chickpea water, also known as aquafaba, is a vegan substitute for eggs. To replace 1 egg white, you need 2 tbsp of chickpea water. Add the chickpea water to a large bowl and beat it into stiff peaks (the same way you would with egg whites). Next add the agave syrup, lemon juice and zest, coconut cream, and the oil. Mix well.

☆ In another bowl, mix together the dry ingredients: buckwheat flour (rich in B vitamins, unlike other gluten-free flours), baking soda, and the pinches of vanilla powder and salt.

☆ Combine the dry and wet ingredients. Pour into a greased mold. Bake for around 30 minutes.

THE COCONUT GLAZE

☆ Mix all of the ingredients together. Once the cake has cooled, remove from the mold, and frost the top of your cake with a spatula.

WITCH'S SECRET

Decorate with candied lemon slices! Just slice a lemon and boil the slices in a solution of 1 part sugar or honey to 2 parts water for 30 minutes. Let dry and arrange them on top of the glazed cake.

# Hormone Balancing
CHOCOLATE BARK

MAKES ENOUGH FOR SEVERAL NIGHTS OF SNACKING · **10 MINUTES + RESTING** · **2–3 MINUTES**

Sometimes our hormonal rhythms guide our food cravings. How can we resist them? More importantly, why should we fight against them? There is an intelligent way to succumb to our desires. Feeling a need for chocolate? It means you probably just need more minerals and magnesium in your diet! Cacao beans are one of the richest sources of magnesium and are filled with antioxidants and essential nutrients and promote hormonal balance. Good-quality dark chocolate is very good for your health and even complexion. And if we add berries and fruits ripe with antioxidants, seeds and nuts rich in omega-3s, and maca and ashwagandha root powders, we will have a chocolate that balances hormones and stimulates the reproductive system. If your hormones are telling you to eat more chocolate, I suggest you listen!

- **14–21 oz (400–600 g)** DARK CHOCOLATE
- **1 TSP** MACA POWDER
- **1 TSP** ASHWAGANDHA POWDER
- BLUEBERRIES
- ½ POMEGRANATE
- DRIED GOJI BERRIES
- RAW PUMPKIN SEEDS
- EDIBLE GOLD DUST OR CACAO POWDER (OPTIONAL)

☆ Melt the chocolate in a water bath and add the maca and ashwagandha powders.

☆ Pour the melted chocolate onto a nonstick baking tray or parchment paper and spread it into an even layer. Sprinkle with berries and seeds, then decorate with gold dust or cacao powder (optional).

☆ Let the tray cool in the refrigerator for a few hours. Break the chocolate into pieces and snack to your heart's (or hormones') content!

WITCH'S SECRET

To help this recipe last longer, use only dried fruits, nuts, and seeds. Replace the blueberries and pomegranate seeds with more shelf-stable macadamia nuts, pistachios, dried figs, dried cranberries, and dried apricots. This version will add energetic powers to this hormone-balancing recipe.

Love APPLES

 MAKES 4 APPLES 15 MINUTES + 30 MINUTES OF RESTING 2-3 MINUTES

The recipe for this traditional carnival treat deserves to be revamped to make it worthy of its French name: *la pomme d'amour,* **or "love apple."** We're going to get a little creative with this autumn apple season dessert. By coating them in a sauce made with natural aphrodisiacs like dates and chocolate, we will increase libido and fertility. Only then can they truly be called love apples. And what would love be without a healthy heart? The fiber in these fruits reinforces proper heart and artery function and removes bad cholesterol from the blood. As for the natural sugars, minerals, and iron found in the dried fruits, they will provide you with a major energy boost. A caramelized treat made with only fruit and dark chocolate—now *that* is self-love.

- 5 oz (150 g) DRIED DATES, PITTED
- 8½ FL OZ (25 CL) WATER
- 3 oz (80 g) DARK CHOCOLATE

- 2 TSP COCONUT CREAM
- PINCH OF SALT
- 4 APPLES

- 4 SMALL STICKS

☆ Place the dates (pitted) in a small bowl and cover with 8½ fl oz (25 cl) of boiling water. Let soften for 30 minutes. Keep the date water! (See the witch's secret at the end of this recipe).

☆ In the meantime, melt the chocolate in a water bath (au bain marie). Remove the dates from the water, place them in a medium-sized bowl, and add the coconut cream and a little salt. Use an immersion blender to turn the dates into a creamy puree.

☆ Next add the melted dark chocolate and salt to the date sauce and mix well.

☆ Remove the stem from each apple (do not peel the apples) and insert a stick in its place. Dip each apple in the chocolate date sauce and let them set on parchment paper.

☆ If the sauce becomes too stiff to adhere to the apples, reheat it in the water bath for a few minutes.

☆ You can serve these immediately or refrigerate them for up to 2 days.

WITCH'S SECRET

You can keep the date water to use in other recipes. It is sweet and rich in the minerals and vitamins found in this magic fruit. Try adding it to herbal teas as a sweetener and healing syrups.

Love CAKE

 SERVES 4–8 · 35 MINUTES · 45 MINUTES

Chocolate cake is one of our most beloved desserts. So, imagine if it could show you some love in return . . . The magic comes from beets and dark chocolate—both of which are rich in aphrodisiac powers—and ground almonds, which balance sex hormones thanks to their vitamin E content. The Aztec emperor Moctezuma was known to drink hot chocolate in order to satisfy his many mistresses. For more on the aphrodisiac powers of beets and chocolates see my Chocolate Aphrodisiac Elixir (p. 156).

- 14 OZ (400 G) DARK CHOCOLATE
- 5 OZ (150 G) ORGANIC HONEY
- 4 EGGS
- ½ TSP OF VANILLA SEEDS OR 1/2 TSP VANILLA EXTRACT
- 7 OZ (200 G) GOAT MILK YOGURT
- 9 OZ (250 G) COOKED BEETS
- 4 OZ (120 G) GROUND ALMONDS
- 3 TBSP CACAO POWDER

- 2 TSP BAKING POWDER
- PINCH OF SALT
- OIL FOR THE MOLDS

FOR THE CHOCOLATE GANACHE

- 17½ OZ (500 G) DARK CHOCOLATE
- 17½ OZ (500 G) ORGANIC CREAM CHEESE (ROOM TEMPERATURE)

- ¾ OZ (20 G) ORGANIC HONEY
- PINCH OF SALT
- POMEGRANATE SEEDS FOR DECORATION

☆ Preheat oven to 350°F (180°C).

☆ Melt the chocolate in a water bath (au bain marie) then pour it into a large bowl. Add the honey and eggs and whisk together. Next incorporate the vanilla and goat milk yogurt. Blend the beets into a puree and add to the chocolate mixture.

☆ In another bowl, mix together the ground almonds, cacao powder, baking powder, and salt. Add to the chocolate mixture and stir well.

☆ Grease two molds and fill them with equal amounts of batter. Bake each cake for 40 minutes: they should be firm to the touch but quite moist on the inside. Stick a knife in each one to test: When you pull it out there should be a little bit of batter stuck to it.

THE CHOCOLATE GANACHE
☆ While the cake is baking, melt the chocolate in a water bath (*au bain marie*) and blend together with the cream cheese. Add the honey and pinch of salt.

☆ Once both cakes are out of the oven, cooled, and removed from their molds, pipe a layer of ganache onto the first cake. Repeat with the second cake and place it on top of the first. Cover with the remaining ganache and use a spatula to smooth everything out. Decorate with pomegranate seeds—they are fertility treasures thanks to their antioxidants.

WITCH'S SECRET

To enhance this cake's aphrodisiac effects, just add 1 small spoonful of maca powder to the batter. And for an extra energy boost, maybe in your morning coffee, too . . .

Matcha Energy
BALLS

⋅⋰⋱ 🍽 | MAKES 20–30 BALLS ⏱ 30 MINUTES ⋰⋱⋅

You know that feeling when your blood sugar drops, you feel exhausted and hungry, but the day is far from over? To conquer these sudden slumps, here's a quick and magical solution that can be eaten in a single bite. These matcha energy balls are made with cashews and ground almonds that are rich in fiber and fatty acid to give you energy all day long, as well as dried dates and apricots rich in iron and vitamin C. But a witch's true talent lies in her ability to intensify the benefits that nature is already offering. To make this recipe even more energizing, we will infuse the cashew nuts in maté tea, a South American herb that contains high levels of caffeine. We'll finish off these treats with a dusting of matcha powder that helps caffeine diffuse slowly and consistently so you can enjoy its benefits all day long, without feeling wired. You can have these energy balls as an afternoon snack, before or after working out, or whenever you're feeling a little hungry!

- 3½ oz **(100 G)** CASHEW NUTS
- 1 TSP MATÉ TEA
- 4½ oz **(125 G)** DRIED APRICOTS

- 3½ oz **(100 G)** DRIED DATES
- ⅓ oz **(10 G)** AGAVE SYRUP OR ORGANIC HONEY

- 2 oz **(50 G)** ALMOND FLOUR
- ⅓ oz **(10 G)** MATCHA POWDER

☆ Place the cashews in a bowl with boiling water and a tea infuser filled with the maté tea (using a tea infuser is easiest). Infuse for 15 minutes.

☆ Drain the cashews and return them to the emptied bowl. Add all of the other ingredients, except the matcha, and blend the mixture into a puree using an immersion blender. Pour the matcha into a small bowl. Wet your hands and form small balls with the fruit and nut mixture. Place the matcha powder on a plate and roll the energy balls through the powder until they are entirely coated.

☆ You can keep these energy balls in the refrigerator for several weeks.

WITCH'S SECRET

If you're a chocolate addict, you can also roll the balls in matcha powder mixed with 1 spoonful of cacao powder. Chocolate has tremendous energetic value. Just one more excuse to enjoy it without overthinking!

137

Chocolate Cake
FOR RADIANT SKIN

 ❙❘❙ SERVES 4–6 🕐 20 MINUTES 📺 40 MINUTES ❙❘❙

Witches know that chocolate possesses countless virtues, but did you know that it is particularly good for your skin's health and beauty? Cacao beans are rich in antioxidants that protect skin from the sun's rays, pollution, and premature aging. Chocolate also makes skin glow, and its effects can be maximized if we marry this magic seed with other foods. Sweet potato and mango are rich in beta-carotene (vitamin A), which participates in collagen synthesis, and mixing sweet potato's rich natural sugars with cacao produces creamy chocolate. So, eat this cake without feeling guilty—taking care of your skin is a good enough excuse!

FOR THE CHOCOLATE-SWEET POTATO CAKE

- 5 OZ (150 G) SWEET POTATO
- 14 OZ (400 G) DARK CHOCOLATE
- 7 OZ (200 G) YOGURT
- 3½ TBSP (5 CL) SUNFLOWER OIL
- 7 OZ (200 G) AGAVE SYRUP
- 3½ OZ (100 G) FLOUR (OR GLUTEN-FREE FLOUR)
- 2 OZ (50 G) CACAO POWDER
- PINCH OF SALT
- BUTTER AND FLOUR FOR THE MOLDS

FOR THE MANGO GANACHE

- ½ MANGO
- 5 OZ (150 G) CASHEW NUTS
- 7 OZ (200 G) MASCARPONE
- 3.5 OZ (100 G) AGAVE SYRUP
- PINCH OF VANILLA POWDER
- A FEW PHYSALIS (EDIBLE FRUIT) FOR DECORATION

THE CHOCOLATE-SWEET POTATO CAKE

☆ Preheat the oven to 350°F (180°C).

☆ Boil the sweet potato until tender. Drain the water. Return to the heat for around 1 minute to dry them out, turning often.

☆ Melt the chocolate in a water bath (au bain marie) and mix with the sweet potato. Next add the yogurt (rich in anti-inflammatory properties to combat acne), the sunflower oil (rich in vitamin E, an essential antioxidant for the skin), and the agave syrup. Mix well.

☆ In a small bowl, mix the flour with the cacao powder and salt. Add these dry ingredients to the wet ingredients and mix.

☆ Butter and two molds and fill them with equal amounts of batter. Bake each cake for 15 minutes. The outside should be golden, and the inside should be moist.

THE MANGO GANACHE

☆ Mix the mango flesh and cashews in a blender to make a puree. Add the mascarpone, agave, and vanilla and mix until you obtain a creamy texture.

☆ Add a thin layer of mango ganache to the tops of each cake layer, and then place one on top of the other before preceding to frost the outside of the cake with the rest of the ganache. Decorate with physalis, a fruit rich in vitamins A and C that will brighten the skin.

WITCH'S SECRET

The ganache can also be served by itself in small glasses like a pudding. This spell is so healthy and delicious it could be its own dessert.

WITCH'S SECRET

If you have overripe avocados, peel, remove the pit, and freeze them for the day you make this recipe or my Waking the Dead Potion (p. 168). Using defrosted avocados works perfectly well, so let's limit as much food waste as we can.

Fertility
CAKE

 SERVES 4–6 15 MINUTES 30 MINUTES

Many nutrients play a role in healthy reproductive system function. How can we be sure we're eating all the vitamins and minerals we need to boost our fertility or simply balance hormones? Just eat all the nutrients together in a cake! This fertility cake is made with avocado, virgin coconut oil, sunflower oil, and goat milk yogurt, all of which are rich in omega-3 fatty acids. Fat is essential for fertility, just as folic acid is important for cell development during pregnancy. Eggs provide a source of complete protein, buckwheat flour offers B vitamins that are essential during pregnancy (and in low supply in other gluten-free flours), and the high concentration of vitamin E in the ground almonds increases fertility and hormone balance in both men and women. In addition to its many nutritional benefits, this cake is incredibly indulgent despite being plant-based. For the best results, eat this cake *without* moderation!

FOR THE CAKE

- ½ AVOCADO
- 3 EGGS
- 1½ OZ (40 G) SUNFLOWER OIL
- 1½ OZ (40 G) VIRGIN COCONUT OIL
- 1 TSP LEMON JUICE
- 3½ OZ (100 G) GOAT MILK YOGURT

- 9 OZ (250 G) HONEY
- 5 OZ (150 G) BUCKWHEAT FLOUR
- 3½ OZ (100 G) GROUND ALMONDS
- 2 TSP BAKING SODA
- 2 TSP BAKING POWDER
- PINCH OF SALT
- OIL FOR THE MOLD

FOR THE COCONUT GLAZE

- 7 TBSP (10 CL) COCONUT CREAM
- 2¼ OZ (60 G) POWDERED SUGAR
- ½ TSP LEMON JUICE
- PISTACHIOS FOR DECORATION

THE CAKE

☆ Preheat the oven to 350°F (180°C).

☆ In a bowl, mix together the avocado, eggs, oils, lemon juice, goat milk yogurt, and honey. In another bowl, combine the remaining dry ingredients and then add them to the wet ingredients. Pour the batter into a greased cake mold.

☆ Bake for 30 minutes: the cake should be golden on the outside, but soft to the touch.

THE COCONUT GLAZE

☆ Separate any liquid from the coconut cream (save it for other recipes!), keeping only the solid part. Place the separated cream in a bowl with the powdered sugar and lemon juice and mix well. Pour the glaze over the cake and when it has set, decorate with chopped pistachio nuts.

Chocolate Pear
CLOUD CAKES

 MAKES 10 MINI FONDANT CAKES OR 1 CAKE (SERVES 4–6)   25 MINUTES   12 MINUTES

When you're in the mood for a snack as light as air that also satisfies your sweet tooth, these little fondant cakes are just what you need. Even better, they're made without gluten, lactose, and processed sugar! Get ready to start baking them every day, because these cakes are as perfect for breakfast as they are for dessert. Incorporating this little cloud into your diet will not only bring you joy, but many health benefits, too. Pears are particularly rich in fiber that fortifies the digestive system, lowers levels of bad cholesterol, and supports heart health. Like pears, chocolate is filled with antioxidants that protect the body from the onslaught of everyday life. These cakes offer long-term energy thanks to the eggs in the recipe (a source of complete protein containing all of the amino acids we need), and the sunflower oil and coconut cream provide omega-3 fatty acids.

- **4** PEARS (OR **10½** OZ [**300** G] PEAR PURÉE)
- **7** OZ (**200** G) MILK CHOCOLATE
- **3½** OZ (**100** G) DARK CHOCOLATE
- **4** EGGS

- **7** OZ (**200** G) HONEY
- **5** TBSP (**7** CL) SUNFLOWER OIL
- **5** TBSP (**7** CL) COCONUT CREAM
- **1** OZ (**30** G) BUCKWHEAT OR RICE FLOUR

- **3½** OZ (**100** G) COCOA POWDER
- **¼** TSP BAKING SODA
- OIL FOR THE MOLD

☆ Preheat the oven to 350°F (180°C).

☆ Peel the pears, slice them into quarters, and remove the seeds. Place the pear quarters in a saucepan with a little bit of water. Cover the pan and boil for 10 minutes: The pears should be tender and almost falling apart. Remove them from the water and place in a large bowl. Either mash the pears with a fork or puree with an immersion blender.

☆ Melt the dark and milk chocolate in a water bath (*au bain marie*) and mix together with the pears. Then add the eggs, honey, sunflower oil, and coconut cream and mix well. Next, combine the flour, cocoa powder, and baking soda in a separate bowl and then fold them into the wet batter and mix well.

☆ Pour the batter into small greased fondant molds (you can also opt for 1 large cake). Bake for 10 minutes (or 30 minutes for a larger cake mold).

WITCH'S SECRET

You can replace the pear puree with apple or banana puree! Or swap in any kind of overripe fruit you have on hand. This will help avoid waste.

Fertility Infusion (see recipe on p. 160)

Potions

⟶❊ MAGIC YOU CAN DRINK ❊⟵

Nature is the cradle of healing magic. This magic is, of course, most concentrated in plants and herbs. You just have to know how to transform them to extract their healing powers. Another of the witch's many talents is turning these natural ingredients into healing potions. Elixirs for strength, love, and sleep do exist outside of fairy tales, and we can find their therapeutic ingredients in forests and fields in the form of flowers and roots. Thanks to the ancient knowledge passed down between witches, we know how to infuse, decoct, and combine these ingredients to extract the full potential of their magical properties. For witches, magic and medicine are intertwined. Whether you need a potion for energy, immunity, detox, relaxation, recovering from or protecting against illness, the magical possibilities are as limitless as the number of healing plants and ingredients found on earth. And sometimes we feel the effects of a potion (when we are searching for sleep or energy, for example) much more quickly than those of a culinary spell (this is because many culinary spells should be regularly consumed before you noticeably feel the benefits). Being in tune with your emotions and health—truly knowing yourself inside and out and how to respond to your body's needs—is the real source of healing potions' power.

Potions GUIDE

Practicing magic is not just a question of being able to identify plants and herbs—you have to know what to do with them. This is the key. If you don't properly prepare plants for a spell, some of the magic may be lost. There are several ways to extract the healing properties from plants, and some parts of the plant need to be treated in a particular way so that these benefits are not destroyed by the extraction process itself. Very often, however, we can concoct the same potion in several ways. The art of alchemy is not an exact science; everything revolves around your instincts.

We prepare infusions to extract medicinal properties from leaves and flowers. These fragile plant parts need to be handled delicately. Place the flowers or leaves in a mug and boil water in a pot. Once the water is boiling, remove it from the heat and pour it over the plants. Cover the mug and let the mixture infuse for at least 20 minutes. You can also let it infuse overnight to make an even more powerful potion.

INFUSIONS

DECOCTIONS

To extract therapeutic properties from roots, bark, or other hard plant parts, you will need a decoction. Hard boil these hard parts directly in a pot of boiling water for at least 20 minutes. Remove the potion from heat and cover to let the healing properties continue to infuse into the water for another 20 minutes.

TINCTURES

To create a potion stronger than most, try a tincture. They require more time and patience, but it's worth it. All plant parts can be used in this method. Prepare a large glass jar with a lid. Cut the plants into small pieces and place them in the jar. Add a few spoonsful of boiling water to help the plants open and release their benefits. Then, fill the jar to the top with high-proof alcohol, vinegar (like organic apple cider vinegar), or food-grade vegetable glycerin. Let the tincture infuse in a cool, dark place for at least two weeks. Shake the jar about every few days. When the tincture has infused to your desired strength, strain the liquid. Take 1–2 tbsp daily as needed. Of course, this takes time, but your patience will be rewarded.

Matcha
FERTILITY POTION

 SERVES 1 5–10 MINUTES (INFUSION)

Maintaining control of your body and, more specifically, your fertility, is as easy as drinking this magic latte every morning. This is the first step toward a more balanced hormonal system, which plays an integral role in everything from immunity to stress levels. Matcha tea (made from young green tea leaves that are grown in the shade) contains ten times the amount of antioxidants as regular green tea. These antioxidants stimulate ovulation and help prevent chromosomal abnormalities that could potentially lead to a miscarriage. To this matcha we will add maca and ashwagandha powders (two adaptogenic roots that stimulate fertility by balancing hormones) and cinnamon and star anise that will reinforce the other ingredients' medicinal magic by supporting regular menstrual cycles. Drinking this potion in the morning will stimulate fertility and also give you a long-term energy boost without feeling wired. And it's definitely more therapeutic than chain drinking espresso!

- 8½ FL OZ (25 CL) ALMOND (OR ANY) MILK
- ¼ TSP MACA POWDER
- ¼ TSP ASHWAGANDHA POWDER

- ⅛ TSP GROUND CINNAMON OR 1 CINNAMON STICK
- 3 STAR ANISE PODS
- 2 TSP VIRGIN COCONUT OIL

- 7 TBSP (10 CL) WATER
- 1 TSP MATCHA POWDER
- 1 TSP HONEY

Fill a small saucepan with the almond milk and add all of the ingredients except the matcha and honey. Let the spices infuse in the milk for 10 minutes.

While the milk absorbs the benefits of these elements, pour the matcha into a small bowl and add 7 tbsp (10 cl) of boiling water. Mix thoroughly with a whisk or fork until the powder is completely absorbed.

Remove the milk from the heat and add the matcha and honey. Drink the latte hot or cold, morning or afternoon, to promote hormonal balance and fertility. You will also benefit from renewed energy, immunity, and anti-inflammation.

WITCH'S SECRET

Drink matcha 1 hour after waking up and not before. Our hormones are hard at work making us feel alert and awake in the morning, so it's best to wait for hormone levels to drop before consuming caffeinated drinks.

Dreamland
POTION

 SERVES 1 20 MINUTES (INFUSION)

Using nature's magic, we can find the good in difficult moments. We can turn nightmares into calming dreams and this transformative power is found in many plants and herbs. Thanks to witches' knowledge, we know how to infuse and blend flowers and roots to extract their magical properties. Sleeping potions are some of the most ancient spells, but helping you fall into a peaceful sleep is only a fraction of what the magic of this potion provides. Flowers like lavender and chamomile are filled with powers connected to the lunar and solar cycles, and matcha and blue lotus flower powders will bewitch your dreams. Together these magical plants stimulate sleep waves in the brain that can induce a feeling of euphoria, more vivid dreams, and deeper sleep.

- **8½ FL OZ (25 CL)** WATER
- **½ TSP** BLUE LOTUS FLOWER POWDER
- **½ TSP** MATCHA POWDER OR **1 TSP** MATCHA LEAVES
- **1 TBSP** CHAMOMILE FLOWERS
- **½ TSP** LAVENDER FLOWERS
- **⅛ OZ (5 G)** ORGANIC HONEY

Boil around 8½ fl oz (25 cl) of water. Place all of the flowers in a mug or heat-resistant glass. As soon as the water begins to boil, remove it from heat and pour over the flowers.

Cover the mug so the flowers can infuse for at least 20 minutes. You can also let them infuse overnight for a more powerful potion.

Filter the potion, add the honey, and drink thirty minutes before going to bed to travel deeper into your dreams.

WITCH'S SECRET

Looking for other ways to intensify your dreams? For a more rapid and potent effect, you can also smoke these magical ingredients. Crush the chamomile and lavender flowers, mix them with the blue lotus powder, then roll them in a cigarette or use in a vaporizer. This technique is used by aboriginal tribes all over the world. The flowers' magic enters the blood immediately without having to pass through the digestive system and you will be able to fall asleep quickly.

Anti-Inflammatory
GOLDEN MILK

 SERVES 1   20 MINUTES (INFUSION)

In one way or another, general inflammation is connected to almost all illnesses that threaten equilibrium in the body. This soothing potion is steeped in the magic of Ayurveda. Here we use roots and spices associated with this ancient Indian medicinal system to neutralize inflammation: turmeric, ginger, cloves, cinnamon, and pepper, which all have powerful therapeutic effects. But as we know, healing magic takes time. Pharmaceutical solutions may have almost instantaneous results, but they treat the symptoms rather than the causes. The magic in this potion helps reestablish the body's equilibrium to better fight inflammation, so try and integrate this into your daily routine. Once you've tasted it, this shouldn't be difficult.

- 8½ FL OZ (25 CL) ALMOND (OR ANY) MILK
- ⅓ OZ (10 G) FRESH TURMERIC OR ½ TBSP GROUND TURMERIC
- ½ OZ (15 G) FRESH GINGER OR ½ TSP GROUND GINGER
- 2 CINNAMON STICKS OR ½ TSP GROUND CINNAMON
- ¼ TSP CLOVES
- ⅛ TSP CAYENNE PEPPER
- ¼ TSP BLACK PEPPER
- ⅙–⅓ OZ (5–10 G) HONEY

Place all of the ingredients except the honey in a saucepan and boil gently for 15 minutes. Filter the potion (you can keep the leftover roots and spices and reuse them when making this potion again, just add a few more fresh ingredients). Add the honey to bring out all of the medicinal properties of this sweet delight.

Drink this potion in the morning or at night to benefit from its anti-inflammatory powers. As is often the case with plant magic, you will have to integrate this treatment for several weeks to feel the full potential of these ingredients!

WITCH'S SECRET

During hot summer months, let this potion cool after infusing the ingredients and serve with ice cubes and a dusting of cinnamon before drinking. We need anti-inflammatory spells all year long.

Detox
SOUP

 SERVES 4   45 MINUTES (INFUSION)

Cabbage is an earth food whose medicinal magic is too often neglected even though it has incredible detoxification powers. Red cabbage in particular is loaded with minerals, calcium, vitamin K, vitamin A (beta-carotene), powerful antioxidants (reflected in the cabbage's purple-red coloring), and anti-inflammatory properties. But most importantly, it is one of the best foods for counteracting the effects of a buildup of toxins. It supports the natural detox mechanisms of the liver and kidneys, helps clean the blood, and is such a powerful diuretic that you must be careful not to drink too much of this potion: Overuse of diuretics (during a weeklong juice fasting-detox regimen, for example) can drain the body of electrolytes that will need to be replenished. To maximize the benefits of cabbage, we can mix it with beets to stimulate the liver as well as onions and celery for a dose of antioxidants. Together, these magical foods create a bright purple potion that cleanses and revitalizes the body while restoring its mineral supply. Don't be surprised if this potion colors your insides. That's just a sign that the cabbage magic is doing its work.

- ½ LARGE HEAD RED CABBAGE OR 1 SMALL HEAD
- 3 BEETS
- 2 ONIONS
- 3 CELERY STALKS

- ⅓ OZ **(10 G)** FRESH GINGER, GRATED
- 1 TBSP APPLE CIDER VINEGAR
- SALT AND PEPPER

WITCH'S SECRET

You can reuse the vegetables in a healing cabbage and beet puree (p. 28).

🝕 Chop the cabbage, beets, onions, and celery into pieces roughly the same size.

🝕 Place the vegetables in a large pot and cover with water. Add the grated ginger and apple cider vinegar. Boil the potion for 45 minutes until all the color has left the vegetables and entered the water.

🝕 Filter the potion. Season with salt and pepper to taste. (Save the vegetables! See the witch's secret for this recipe on how to use them.)

Relaxing Flower ELIXIR

 🍷 SERVES 4   🕐 20 MINUTES (INFUSION)

There are ways to treat stress and anxiety that are healthier and more natural than traditional medications, which may have side effects. Where can we find them? In many plants, but particularly in flowers. We can make an elixir using passionflower, which has a calming effect on brain activity, valerian root, the plant origin of Valium, and lavender, a reliever of nervous tension and emotional stress that calms the autonomic nervous system. Doesn't that sound more inviting? To extract the magical properties of these plants, first brew the flowers in an infusion and then prepare a decoction with the valerian root. Unlike delicate flowers whose powers would be destroyed by a decoction, hard roots need to be boiled.

- 2 TBSP PASSIONFLOWER
- ½ TBSP LAVENDER
- 8½ FL OZ (25 CL) WATER
- 1 TBSP VALERIAN ROOT
- ⅓ OZ (10 G) ORGANIC HONEY

Place the passionflower and lavender in a mug or heat-resistant glass.

Bring about 8½ fl oz (25 cl) of water to a boil and remove immediately from heat before pouring over the flowers. Cover the mug so the flowers can infuse for at least 20 minutes.

You can also make this potion in advance and let the flowers infuse overnight for a more powerful effect. While the flower magic starts to do its work, make a decoction with the valerian root.

When you have extracted enough power from the plants, mix them together. Drink this elixir—after adding the honey—whenever you feel stressed, and after a few minutes you should start to feel the relaxing magic of flowers blossoming within you.

WITCH'S SECRET

Sometimes when we are particularly stressed, we need an almost immediate solution. In moments like these, we can transform this recipe into a tincture, which will do an even better job than hot water at extracting the magical benefits. Place all of the ingredients in a jar with apple cider vinegar or high-proof alcohol and infuse for at least 2 weeks. Filter the tincture and take 1–2 tbsp a day during times of extreme stress.

Chocolate
APHRODISIAC ELIXIR

 SERVES 1   10 MINUTES (INFUSION)

Magic should never "force" someone to fall in love, but we can bend the rules a little by creating a potion that increases desire. Certain aphrodisiac ingredients affect not only our sexual appetite but our physical endurance as well. Maca increases the production of sex hormones, and beet juice generates nitric oxide, which increases physical capacity, blood flow, and . . . performance. Lastly, I have included chocolate, the aphrodisiac ingredient par excellence that brings us back to the magic of the Aztecs.

- **3** RAW BEETS
- **2** OZ **(50 G)** DARK CHOCOLATE
- **1** TSP MACA POWDER

Juice the beets until you have around 7 fluid ounces (20 cl) of liquid. If you don't have a juicer, you can use juice from precooked beets.

Melt the chocolate together with the beet juice in a small saucepan over low heat.

Now add the maca powder. Cook gently for 5 minutes.

Drink this elixir *without* moderation to stimulate your libido.

WITCH'S SECRET

You can also add a grating of ginger and a pinch of cayenne pepper to amplify the libido-stimulating magic of the other ingredients!

Bone BROTH

   SERVES 4–6   3 HOURS (DECOCTION)

Animal bones have phenomenal powers. The collagen found in bone and marrow is the most abundant protein in the body, is rich in amino acids that support immunity and digestive health, reduces general inflammation, promotes weight stability, and fortifies our muscles, skin, and bones. Animal bones also contain a wide range of essential minerals. This spell is also very eco-friendly because it uses what we would normally throw away: meat bones and poultry carcasses, vegetable skins and roots. . . This is a potion that supports both the body's equilibrium and the health of the earth and goes hand in hand with the values of culinary magic.

- CHICKEN CARCASS AND MEAT BONES
- **2** ONIONS AND THEIR SKINS
- **1** WHOLE LEEK OR GREEN PARTS FROM **1** LEEK
- **3½** OZ **(100** G) MUSHROOMS
- **3–4** GARLIC CLOVES AND THEIR SKINS
- HERBS (PARSLEY, ROSEMARY, THYME)
- ANY ROOT VEGETABLES OR LEFTOVER SCRAPS
- SALT AND PEPPER
- **68** FL OZ **(2** LITERS) WATER

Place all of the ingredients in a pot filled with 68 fl oz (2 liters) of water and cover.

Boil the bone potion for at least 3 hours to extract the magic hidden in the bones and earth elements.

Add water during cooking if needed. Drink the broth immediately or freeze it. Eat the leftover vegetables alone or with grains.

WITCH'S SECRET

Keep a bag in the freezer where you can store leftover bones and vegetables. When you have enough, transform them into bone broth. You can also ask your butcher to give you any bones that would normally be thrown away.

159

Fertility
INFUSION

  SERVES 1 15 MINUTES (INFUSION)

Are you looking for an easy way to maintain hormonal balance and increase your fertility? Drink a combination of flowers and leaves from magical fruits with a little royal jelly. The clary sage flowers will help stabilize hormones and the red raspberry leaf will help tone the uterus. Royal jelly is particularly useful for stimulating ovulation, and this infusion can reinvigorate the body before childbirth. That's right: Nature hides her fertility magic in flowers, fruits, and bee nectar! The queen bee is exclusively fed royal jelly (a substance secreted from nurse bees that is also given to bee larvae) so she can lay eggs for the entire colony. In nature, bees, flowers, and their fruits are the foundation of the cycle of creation.

- 8½ FL OZ **(25 CL)** WATER
- **2** TBSP RED RASPBERRY LEAF
- **2** TBSP CLARY SAGE FLOWERS
- ⅓ OZ **(10 G)** ROYAL JELLY

WITCH'S SECRET

Other magical plants that support fertility: ashwagandha, maca, parsley, mugwort, vitex, yarrow, dandelion, marshmallow, red clover, cinnamon, echinacea, ginger, and nettle. Always consult a doctor before integrating plant medicine while pregnant or nursing.

🫙 Boil 8½ fl oz (25 cl) of water and pour it into a mug with the red raspberry leaf and clary sage flowers. Cover the mug and infuse for 15 minutes.

🫙 Filter and add the royal jelly. Drink this infusion before bedtime.

Fire
CIDER

  MAKES ENOUGH FOR 2 WEEKS TO 1 MONTH OF TREATMENT

 1 WEEK TO 1 MONTH (TINCTURE)

This fire cider is going to perk your body up in many ways. Witches have had this remedy for centuries and use it to improve energy, boost immunity, and restore the digestive system. This may not be the best-tasting potion you'll ever try, but it makes up for its fiery taste with its healing properties. This magical elixir helps balance blood sugar, cholesterol, and blood pH, nourishes the gut microbiota, and kills harmful bacteria. The apple cider vinegar used as the base of this potion can even help the body burn fat more efficiently. The fresh ginger and turmeric infused in the vinegar counteracts general inflammation and improves blood circulation. Onion, black radish, and garlic raise immunity and are rich in antioxidants. The nutrient-dense citrus offers balance, pepper helps the body absorb the entire potion's benefits, and manuka honey is rich in immunostimulant and antibacterial properties. Drink this cider whenever you're feeling weak or as an elixir of protection. It's worth it!

- ½ BLACK RADISH
- ¾–1 OZ (20–30 G) FRESH GINGER
- ½–¾ OZ (15–20 G) FRESH TURMERIC
- 4 SMALL ONIONS

- 2–3 GARLIC CLOVES JUICE OF 1 ORANGE + ITS PEEL
- JUICE OF 1 LEMON + ITS PEEL
- 2–4 SMALL CAYENNE PEPPER SEEDS (OR 1 TSP GROUND CAYENNE PEPPER)

- 1 TSP BLACK PEPPER
- ¾–1½ OZ (20–40 G) MANUKA HONEY
- 17 FL OZ (50 CL) ORGANIC APPLE CIDER VINEGAR

🧴 Slice the black radish, ginger, and turmeric. Peel the onions and garlic and cut them in half. Place these and all remaining ingredients in a glass jar and fill with vinegar.

🧴 Keep the jar sealed for at least 2 weeks so the benefits of the ingredients can infuse the vinegar. When the cider is infused to your desired strength, filter the contents of the jar.

🧴 Drink 1–2 tbsp (15–30 ml) per day as needed or as a preventive measure to stimulate the immune system.

WITCH'S SECRET

To sweeten the taste, add hibiscus flowers and raw beets.

Digestive Repair
LATTE

  SERVES 1   15 MINUTES (INFUSION)

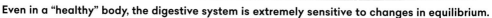

Even in a "healthy" body, the digestive system is extremely sensitive to changes in equilibrium. The stomach and colon have a huge job to do and need a great deal of energy to digest our food, absorb the vitamins, minerals, and enzymes the body needs to function, and eliminate all of the bad elements. This mechanism is working almost nonstop and sometimes needs a boost. Cardamom, ginger, star anise, fennel, cumin, and licorice root form an infusion that reinforces digestive balance. This potion stimulates and assists the digestive system before or after a meal. The spices steeped in anti-inflammatory milk help rebalance gastric acid and ease heartburn and spasms. A healthy digestive system will support all the other functions of the body.

- **5** FL OZ **(15** CL) ALMOND, OAT, HEMP, OR GOAT MILK
- **3–5** CARDAMOM PODS
- ½ TSP FENNEL SEEDS
- ⅛ OZ **(5** G) FRESH GINGER, GRATED

- **3** STAR ANISE PODS
- SMALL PINCH OF GROUND CUMIN
- **1** LICORICE ROOT STICK (OR **3** EXTRA STAR ANISE PODS)

Place all of the ingredients in a saucepan and heat to a gentle boil. Then lower the heat and infuse for 15 minutes.

Filter the liquid (you can keep the spices for future potions) and drink this potion in the morning or before or after dinner to calm and repair the digestive system.

WITCH'S SECRET

Add a pinch of black pepper. This spice will help the body better absorb the other nutrients and maintain gut microbiota equilibrium.

Sleeping Flowers
ELIXIR

 SERVES 1   15 MINUTES (INFUSION)

Treat yourself to a nighttime drink far more enchanting than herbal tea. For a creative and floral potion that transmits the magic of tranquility plants, infuse almond milk with chamomile and lavender flowers. The calcium and magnesium in almond milk will facilitate the creation of melatonin, and cinnamon pairs perfectly with the delicate flavor of the flowers to calm the nervous system and muscles for more peaceful sleep. It is best to enjoy the magic of sleeping flowers in a warming potion before bed . . .

- 8½ FL OZ **(25 CL)** ALMOND MILK
- ½ TBSP LAVENDER FLOWERS
- 1 TBSP CHAMOMILE FLOWERS
- 1 TSP CINNAMON
- ½ OZ **(15 G)** ORGANIC HONEY

Warm the milk in a small saucepan over low heat until just before boiling. Remove the milk from the heat, add the flowers and spices, and infuse for 15 minutes.

Filter the potion and add the honey. Drink one hour before going to bed for calmer and deeper sleep.

WITCH'S SECRET

Add a little grated fresh ginger and an extra pinch or two of cinnamon to transform this potion into an evening digestion spell. The digestive system often slows down at night and this can cause stomach pain. The ginger and cinnamon work to soothe the stomach and balance acidity.

Healing Pine
NEEDLE SYRUP

 MAKES 1 BOTTLE (1–2 WEEKS OF TREATMENT)   45 MINUTES (DECOCTION)

> **Trees that can withstand the most extreme weather conditions are the ones that heal and protect us best during the winter months.** Almost every part of the tree possesses medicinal benefits, but for this spell, we are interested in their needles, which are particularly rich in antioxidants (especially vitamin A), boost immunity and red blood cell production, strengthen the skin, and share their anti-inflammatory, antibacterial, and antiviral properties with us. This syrup is perfect for treating winter illnesses because pine needles are also decongestants. They can potentially even help balance your mood and improve your memory. The secret to fighting off the effects of winter? Use winter's own magic as protection!

- **2–3** PINE BRANCHES (WITH PLENTY OF NEW SHOOTS)
- **27** FLUID OZ **(80 CL)** WATER
- **3½** OZ **(100 G)** HONEY

Separate the pine needles from the branches and place them in a pot filled with 27 fluid oz (80 cl) of water. Boil until the water has reduced by half.

Filter and mix the water with the honey.

Transfer the syrup to a sterilized glass bottle or jar, seal, and store, or use right away. Take 2 tbsp 2–3 times daily to treat a cold or the flu.

WITCH'S Secret

Make sure you use true pine needles and not needles from other similar-looking but false pine trees like the Buddhist pine or the Norfolk Island pine. All true pine trees can be eaten, but they have different flavors. Taste the needles to choose the ones you like best and use new shoots for a better flavor.

Immunity Berry
SYRUP

🫙 MAKES ENOUGH FOR 1 WEEK OF TREATMENT

🕐 2 HOURS TO OVERNIGHT (INFUSION)

The elderberry tree offers unparalleled medicinal benefits, particularly for the immune system. These small, dark-purple berries are packed with antioxidants that protect the body from viruses and bacteria. What's more, they stimulate the immune system, neutralize viruses, and keep them from spreading to healthy cells. By drinking this magic syrup, you can reduce the duration of an illness and protect your body during the winter months. The manuka honey, infused herbs, and ginger in this syrup offer your immune system an additional boost.

- **2** oz **(50** g**)** DRIED ELDERBERRIES
- **⅓** oz **(10** g**)** FRESH GINGER
- **17** FL OZ **(50** CL**)** WATER
- **3–5** ROSEMARY SPRIGS
- **3–5** THYME SPRIGS
- **1** OZ **(30** G**)** MANUKA HONEY

🫙 Put the elderberries and grated ginger in a pot with 17 fl oz (50 cl) of water and cover. Boil gently until the water has reduced by half.

🫙 Crush the elderberries with a spoon as they cook to help release their benefits. Remove the pot from the heat and add the sprigs of rosemary and thyme before covering again. Let the potion infuse for 1 hour or overnight.

🫙 The next day, filter the potion. Add the manuka honey.

🫙 Take 4 spoonsful twice a day if you feel under the weather, and 2 spoonsful a day before bed as a preventive measure.

🫙 If you want to make this syrup in advance and store it to use at a later date: The day after you make the potion, reheat it to a boil, then add the manuka honey, and transfer to a sterilized glass jar.

WITCH'S SECRET

Freeze the syrup in a glass or in a popsicle mold as a soothing treat for sore throats.

Waking the
DEAD POTION

🌿 🍷 SERVES 1 ⏱ 5 MINUTES 🌿

Whether you're dizzy, nauseous, or hit with a splitting headache, hangovers can certainly be unpleasant. In these situations, we need a little something to "wake the dead." This enchanting smoothie is concocted using activated charcoal, which relieves nausea and helps detoxify the liver and kidneys, and foods rich in potassium and minerals to rehydrate the body. This elixir also works to counteract general fatigue, exhaustion, and dehydration.

- **1** BANANA
- **1** AVOCADO
- **4½** FL OZ (**13** CL) PINEAPPLE JUICE
- **½** TSP ACTIVATED CHARCOAL
- PINCH OF VANILLA POWDER
- PINCH OF SALT

🧴 Blend all of the ingredients until your mixture has the texture of a smoothie.

🧴 Drink this potion to relieve stomach pain and refuel an exhausted body.

WITCH'S SECRET

To help prevent a hangover and protect your stomach, liver, and kidneys, I suggest drinking this potion *before* consuming potions that are more... alcoholic.

Energy
TINCTURE

  MAKES 1 BOTTLE 2 + WEEKS (TINCTURE)

Energy tinctures are essential potions for the modern world. This one is perfect to help us survive in a society where we are always on the go and where stress and chronic lack of sleep are becoming a norm of daily life. With this potion, we can counteract these immense everyday pressures. Rhodiola, holy basil, maca, and schisandra are adaptogenic herbs that have their roots in Indian magic, more specifically in the practice of Ayurveda. They balance stress hormones and boost energy. This potion, because it comes in the form of an alcohol–or vinegar–based tincture, contains a high concentration of these magical plants. Drink this tincture every morning to support your adrenal system, and if you are experiencing extreme fatigue, take a dose to restore your energy. Unlike with coffee, you won't crash after a few hours and its effects usually last for a long time and help treat burnout with longer-term use.

- **4** TBSP RHODIOLA ROOT
- **4** TBSP BASIL
- **3** TBSP MACA POWDER
- **3** TBSP SCHISANDRA BERRIES
- **10** FL OZ (**30** CL) APPLE CIDER VINEGAR OR HIGH-PROOF ALCOHOL

Add all of the plants to a medium-sized jar and cover with apple cider vinegar or high-proof alcohol. Close the jar and infuse for 2 weeks to 6 months in a cool, dark place.

Shake the jar several times a week. Once it has infused to your desired strength, filter the tincture. Take ½ tbsp per day, then increase by 1 tbsp per week for at least one month and up to three months.

These magical plants are very powerful, and you must ask your physician's advice before taking this tincture with other medications, if you have health problems, or if pregnant or breast feeding.

WITCH'S SECRET

You can also replace the schisandra berries with fresh cranberries. These two berries play the same role in supporting kidney and liver detox.

Immune Boost
TINCTURE

 MAKES ENOUGH FOR 1–2 WEEKS OF TREATMENT 2 + WEEKS (TINCTURE)

Immune-boosting potions are part of the witch's protective arsenal and are particularly import-ant during the long winter months. This infusion uses immune-regulating herbs, plants, and vitamin D–packed medicinal mushrooms whose powers strengthen the body's immune defenses. If you feel yourself coming down with something or want to protect yourself from getting sick, drink this potion every night before bed until your symptoms disappear or for one week if you are in contact with someone who is ill. Respect the plant magic and do not drink this potion over long periods of time—you risk becoming too accustomed to the ingredients.

- **4** SHIITAKE MUSHROOMS
- **5** THYME SPRIGS
- **5** ROSEMARY SPRIGS
- **½** OZ **(15** G) GINGER
- **⅓** OZ **(10** G) ECHINACEA FLOWERS
- **5** SAGE LEAVES

- **3½** TBSP **(5** CL) WATER
- **10** FL OZ **(30** CL) APPLE CIDER VINEGAR OR HIGH-PROOF ALCOHOL OR FOOD GRADE VEGETABLE GLYCERIN
- **⅓** OZ **(10** G) MANUKA HONEY

Chop the mushrooms. Remove the thyme and rosemary leaves. Peel and grate the ginger.

Place all of the ingredients except the manuka honey in a glass jar and cover with 3½ tbsp (5 cl) of boiling water and the vinegar, alcohol, or glycerin. Close the jar.

Let the potion infuse in a dark and cool place for 2 weeks to 3 months. When the potion has infused to your desired strength, filter it. Then add the manuka honey.

Take 1–2 spoonsful twice a day when you feel under the weather, or for 7 days as a protective spell.

WITCH'S SECRET

To increase the power of the shiitake mushrooms, leave them in the sun for one day, gills up, so they can fill up on vitamin D. The magic of shiitake is linked to the sun. And for an even more effective dose of mushroom magic, try reishi mushrooms!

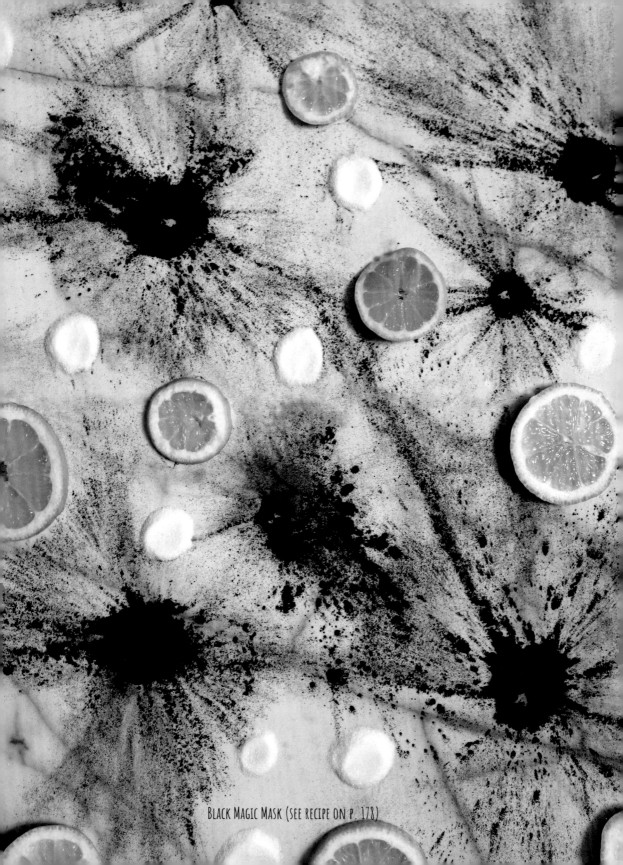

Black Magic Mask (see recipe on p. 178)

Recipes
FOR ETERNAL YOUTH

The idea of using magic from the natural world to heal oneself can also be applied to beauty. Everything is connected, and your health is reflected in your physical appearance. Aging is part of the cycle of life and we should embrace it, not be afraid of it, but that doesn't mean we have to let our body—this magnificent inheritance—wither away while we do nothing. The secret of eternal youth is found in the magic of plants and other natural elements. By understanding their properties and how they interact with the body, we can create natural beauty spells like oils, creams, and elixirs from pure and untreated plants. Why pay a fortune for cosmetics made with unknown production methods and very often toxic chemical substances when you can use foods and eath elements that are inexpensive, safe, and have healing properties? Whatever chemicals you apply to your skin, hair, or nails are absorbed and rapidly diffuse into the blood. If we follow this reasoning, we might as well be ingesting everything we put on our bodies. Makes sense, right?

Witches all submit to the passage of time, but there's no reason they can't slow it down, control the changes in their bodies, and remedy these changes to their desire.

Chamomile
OIL

  MAKES 1–2 JARS 3 HOURS TO 2 WEEKS (INFUSION)

What do we get when we infuse the magic of flowers with the magic of almonds? An anti-inflammatory beauty elixir. General inflammation can affect organs, joints, and muscles, but it can impact the skin as well. Cystic acne, which may pose aesthetic problems, is a particularly painful inflammation of the skin. Chamomile flower not only helps us sleep, but it also soothes the skin with its anti-inflammatory magic. To maximize these effects, we infuse this magic in sweet almond oil, which is rich in antioxidants to help the skin heal and protect it from inflammation. The high levels of reparative vitamin E and A in this oil also fight acne. Preparing the ingredients for this flower oil takes less time than it takes to make chamomile tea. You will just need to add a little fire or sun magic for the infusion to take place.

- 5 FL OZ **(15 CL)** ORGANIC SWEET ALMOND OIL
- ⅛ OZ **(5 G)** DRIED CHAMOMILE FLOWERS

◯ Pour the oil into a glass jar and add the dried chamomile flowers. Infuse the jar directly in a water bath over low heat for at least 3 hours, or, for a slower infusion, place the jar in direct sunlight for at least 1 week.

◯ You can either strain out the flowers and transfer the oil to a glass dropper vial or simply leave the flowers in the jar so they can continue to infuse into the oil. This will make it more powerful over time.

WITCH'S SECRET

Apply this oil to stretch marks to reduce their appearance (this beauty potion is safe for use during pregnancy) and to skin rashes to calm inflammation. It will help protect and repair sensitive skin.

Black Magic
MASK

✦✦✦ ◯◯ MAKES 1 MASK ◷ 5 MINUTES ✦✦✦

This mask is made using black magic because its effects on the skin are too profound to be authorized by the laws of white magic. This spell is carried out in two steps: first, a mixture of activated charcoal and baking soda is applied to the face, and then, after several minutes, lemon juice is added. The mask will then come to life and begin to foam, multiplying the benefits of the first part of the enchantment. Charcoal purifies the skin and absorbs impurities, toxins, and microparticles of pollution. It makes the skin radiant and clear and also fights acne. Baking soda exfoliates, restores the skin's pH, and removes dead cells from the epidermis. The acid from the lemon juice activates the potion. The resulting emulsion cleans and exfoliates the skin on an even deeper level. The effects are so remarkable and immediate that they can only be the work of magical ingredients.

- **1** TSP ACTIVATED CHARCOAL
- ½ TSP BAKING SODA
- ½ TSP LEMON JUICE

⊛ In a small bowl, mix the activated charcoal with the baking soda and add a few drops of water until your paste has an even texture. Apply to the face. Don't forget your neck! Massage gently to exfoliate the skin.

⊛ Leave the mask on for 10 minutes while the mask does its work and the charcoal purifies your skin.

⊛ For the last step, stay close to the sink. Practicing the art of magic can sometimes be a slightly messy affair . . .

⊛ Using a small spoon or dropper, pour the lemon juice onto your face (be careful not to get any in your eyes) and admire the spell as it starts bubbling away! Rinse with warm water.

WITCH'S SECRET

You can also use this mask for your hair. Apply the paste to the scalp for 10 minutes. Add the lemon juice before washing normally.

Natural SUNSCREEN

 MAKES 1 JAR   2 HOURS

Just because a beauty product is sold in the pharmacy or by a well-known brand doesn't necessarily make it high-quality. Most sunscreens contain too many chemical products. Here I'm offering you a natural recipe for a carrot oil infusion that has a total SPF of around 25 that you can combine with shea butter (SPF 6–10) and coconut oil (SPF 7). The high vitamin C levels found in the amla powder also protect from UV ray damage. As is very often the case with magic potions, these ingredients do not have the same effects individually as they do when used simultaneously. In combination, however, they complement each other to protect your skin.

- 2 CARROTS
- 5½ TBSP (8 CL) ORGANIC SWEET ALMOND OIL
- 5½ TBSP (8 CL) VIRGIN COCONUT OIL
- 1 TSP AMLA POWDER OR VITAMIN C POWDER
- ⅓ OZ (10 G) ZINC OXIDE POWDER
- 1 OZ (30 G) BEESWAX
- ¾ OZ (20 G) SHEA BUTTER

Preheat the oven to 195°F (90°C).

Place the grated carrots in a small baking dish and cover with the sweet almond oil and virgin coconut oil.

Cover the dish with aluminum foil. Bake for 2 hours, checking every half hour to make sure there is still enough oil and the carrots aren't burning. Add more oil as needed.

When the carrots have infused long enough, filter the oil. Keep the carrots to use in other recipes like the Candle Illusion Cakes (p. 122).

Transfer the carrot oil to a glass jar and place it in a pot in a water bath (au bain marie), adding the amla or vitamin C powder, zinc oxide powder, beeswax, and shea butter. Stir until the wax has melted.

After the mixture has cooled, place the jar in the refrigerator. Apply the cream before going outside and every 2 hours during sun exposure.

WITCH'S SECRET

Don't have the time to make your own carrot oil? Buy it in the store and use as described in the recipe. Skipping steps isn't always a bad thing . . . If you don't have beeswax either, don't worry: your sunscreen will just be an oil instead of a cream.

Dragon's
BLOOD MASK

❋ 👁 1 MASK   ⏱ 5 MINUTES ❋

Dragon's blood is not a mythical ingredient dreamt up in the realm of fairytales. Before it appeared in the legend of King Arthur, this magical element was used by witches of the forest. It is now an essential part of any modern witch's medicine chest, but this "blood" comes from a mysterious tree with dark-red sap, not a mythical creature. For thousands of years, witches and indigenous tribes have used this ingredient during ceremonies. When the Amazonians were wounded by animals during a hunt, they would cut this magic tree to release the sap and use it to cover their wounds. They knew the sap would immediately stop the bleeding and form a sort of bandage that would help the skin regenerate. Applied as a face mask, this product with many powers repairs damaged cells, reduces wrinkles, and tightens pores even on tired skin. When ingested, dragon's blood also relieves stomach pain and nausea. It purifies the body and can also be used as a toothpaste to treat receding and weak gums. Finding the secret of eternal youth in the blood of a dragon? Now *that* is true magic.

- **5–10** DROPS OF DRAGON'S BLOOD
- **½ TSP** JOJOBA OR ORGANIC SWEET ALMOND OIL
- **½ TSP** HONEY

⊛ Mix all of the ingredients together in a small bowl and apply the mixture to your face.

⊛ Leave the potion on your skin for at least 20 minutes and rinse with warm water. You can also leave it on all day.

⊛ Be careful—dragon's blood is a magical ingredient that stains even more than turmeric!

WITCH'S SECRET

Dragon's blood also relieves digestive problems because of its antibacterial properties. Take a small spoonful of dragon's blood in a glass of water 2–4 times a day to treat stomach discomfort.

Night Elixir
FOR ETERNAL YOUTH

  MAKES 1 SMALL BOTTLE 10 MINUTES

This elixir makes your skin more radiant than any cream can. Certain oils are good at fighting free radicals (like pollution and UV rays) that contribute most to premature skin aging. Sweet almond oil is rich in vitamin E and using this vitamin in its natural form is better than applying a synthetic version in a traditional face cream, for example. Sweet almond oil softens the skin and smooths fine wrinkles. It is also rich in antioxidants that protect the skin from pollution. Geranium oil has the same virtues and was a beauty secret of the geishas, who used the oil to strengthen their hair. Rose oil comes from a magical flower that protects the body from free radicals and is rich in antioxidants and anti-inflammatory properties. What poetry on nature's part to hide beauty secrets in the magic of flowers!

- 3½ TBSP **(5 CL)** ORGANIC SWEET ALMOND OIL
- 3½ TBSP **(5 CL)** GERANIUM OIL
- **4** DROPS OF ROSE ESSENTIAL OIL

WITCH'S SECRET
You can also use this oil on your hair and nails! If you want to try another flower with beauty benefits, I suggest jasmine essential oil.

⊕ Mix all of the ingredients together and pour the oil into a glass bottle.

⊕ Apply the elixir before bed, when the oils' magic will be most effective.

Rejuvenating GREEN MASK

  MAKES 1-2 MASKS 5 MINUTES

One advantage of magic is that it allows us to protect our health and beauty using simple potions made at home. This mask shields your skin from the evils of daily life: pollution and overexposure to the sun, for example. To make this green potion, we use three ingredients that detoxify, protect, and repair: matcha tea powder, which is rich in antioxidants (around twenty times more than blueberries), minerals, vitamins, and skin-nourishing chlorophyll, amla powder with vitamin C to repair and protect the skin from sunburn and repair collagen, and green clay powder, which helps purify the skin by removing micro-molecules and bacteria on acne-prone skin. The real magic happens when these three ingredients are used together.

- ½ TSP GREEN CLAY POWDER
- ½ TSP MATCHA POWDER
- ¼ TSP AMLA OR VITAMIN C POWDER

WITCH'S SECRET

Apply this mask just before stepping into the shower. The humidity will help the mask stay on longer and clean the pores deeply without irritating your skin when the mask dries.

⊛ Mix the clay, matcha, and amla powder (or vitamin C powder) in a small bowl. Add a few drops of water until your paste has an even texture.

⊛ Apply to the neck and face, avoiding the eyes, and leave on for 15 minutes before rinsing with warm water.

Hair-Strengthening
OIL

  MAKES 1–2 JARS 3 HOURS TO 2 WEEKS (INFUSION)

We spend too much time washing our hair and not enough time nourishing and protecting it. It is just as affected by the hostilities of pollution and sun exposure as your skin is, and shampoo and conditioners are all too often loaded with toxic chemical products that can cause long-term damage to your hair and body. This oil-based potion strengthens your hair follicles and scalp tissue. Jojoba oil nourishes hair and is the oil most similar to our skin's sebum. It hydrates and penetrates the hair to deeply nourish it while hibiscus flowers and rosemary essential oil help invigorate the hair follicles, strengthen hair, and destroy bacteria. Apply this mask 2 hours before washing your hair normally and you will be impressed by the magic of these healing oils.

- **4 FL OZ (12 CL)** JOJOBA OR ORGANIC SWEET ALMOND OIL
- **⅓ OZ (10 G)** DRIED HIBISCUS FLOWERS
- **15** DROPS OF ORGANIC ROSEMARY ESSENTIAL OIL
- **10** DROPS OF ORGANIC MINT ESSENTIAL OIL

⊛ Pour the jojoba oil into a small glass jar and add the dried hibiscus flowers. For a quick infusion, heat the jar in a water bath (au bain marie) over low heat for 3 hours. For a slower and therefore more intense infusion, leave the jar of oil in the sun for 1–2 weeks. If you are making this oil in winter and the sun doesn't want to show its face, you can also place the little jar near a heater: the heat will help extract the healing properties from the hibiscus. Once the oil is infused to your desired strength, add the rosemary and mint essential oils and mix.

⊛ Pour a small spoonful of this repairing oil onto your scalp, massage, and let sit for 2 hours before washing your hair normally.

WITCH'S SECRET

If you can't find hibiscus flowers, you can replace them with 10 drops of lavender essential oil or 5 extra drops of rosemary essential oil and 5 extra drops of mint essential oil. Even when we don't have all the right ingredients for a spell, we can always find a substitute!

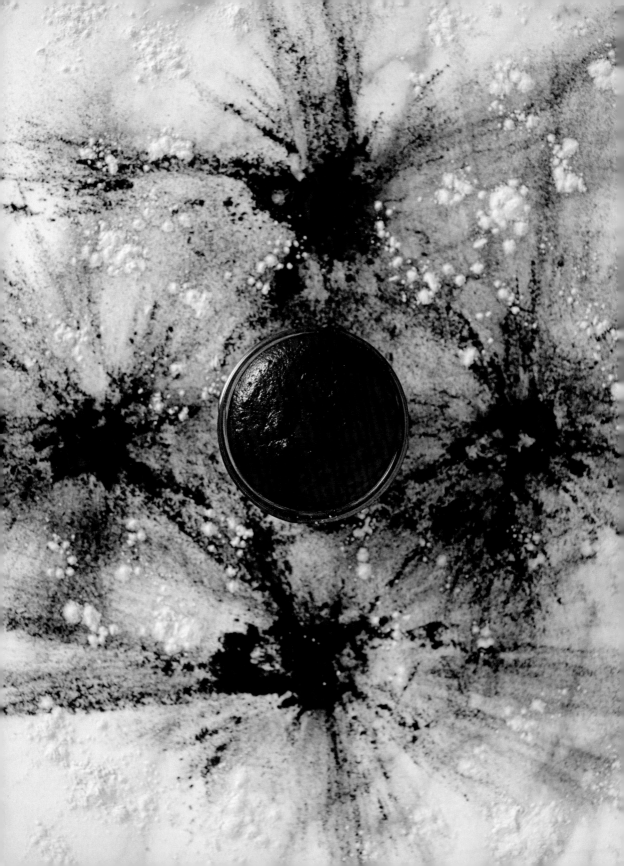

Black Magic
TOOTHPASTE

  MAKES 1 JAR 5 MINUTES

This spell uses black magic to whiten your teeth. But this toothpaste made with activated charcoal has powers that go beyond improving appearance: The charcoal works in tandem with bentonite clay to remove bacteria hiding between your teeth and under the gum line. The baking soda scrubs away tartar and balances saliva pH, and the amla powder (or vitamin C powder) protects the gums from gingivitis. This spell is so effective that you will see (and feel) the difference after just one brushing.

- ¾ OZ (20 G) ACTIVATED CHARCOAL
- ¾ OZ (20 G) BENTONITE CLAY
- 1/6 OZ (5 G) AMLA OR VITAMIN C POWDER
- ⅓ OZ (10 G) BAKING SODA
- 5½ TBSP (8 CL) WATER

WITCH'S SECRET

You can also leave the toothpaste on your teeth for 10 minutes. It will act as a whitening mask.

⊛ Mix all of the ingredients together with 5½ tbsp (8 cl) of water in a glass jar until your mixture has the consistency of toothpaste.

⊛ Brush gently around 20 minutes after every meal.

Pain Relief
CREAM

 🥫 MAKES 1–2 SMALL JARS   🕐 10 MINUTES + 15 MINUTES OF RESTING

The magic of certain natural ingredients offers pain relief with almost no side effects. This is not the case for traditional pain relief creams, which contain extremely powerful ingredients, are often contraindicated for people with certain health conditions and taking certain medications. You can use this natural anti-inflammatory cream for muscular, nerve, or joint pain as often as you like with no risk of side effects. (If you are pregnant or wish to use it on a child under the age of three, ask your physician for advice beforehand).

- ½ OZ **(15 G)** BEESWAX
- **4** TBSP **(6 CL)** VIRGIN COCONUT OR ORGANIC SWEET ALMOND OIL
- ½ OZ **(15 G)** SHEA BUTTER
- **15** DROPS OF ORGANIC TARRAGON ESSENTIAL OIL
- **10** DROPS OF ORGANIC ROSEMARY ESSENTIAL OIL
- **10** DROPS OF ORGANIC EUCALYPTUS ESSENTIAL OIL

⊗ Melt the beeswax in the virgin coconut (or sweet almond) oil along with the shea butter. Next add the essential oils and stir together. Refrigerate to allow the cream to harden.

⊗ Apply to painful areas and massage.

WITCH'S SECRET

When treating muscular or joint pain, make sure you don't have a magnesium deficiency, which could contribute to such discomfort. If this is the case, eat foods that are rich in magnesium like spinach, kale, watercress, avocado, broccoli, cabbage, salmon, nuts, seeds, and dark chocolate!

Shower
SCRUB

 MAKES 1 JAR 5 MINUTES

Store-bought creams and scrubs are expensive, and you can get the same effects with a single spell that will hardly cost you anything. And, because time is as valuable as your health, you can apply it in the shower. This shower scrub is made from magnesium salt that exfoliates the skin, soothes muscles, and calms the nervous system with minerals. Coconut oil is rich in omega-3 fatty acids that hydrate the skin better than creams because they target cells individually. Using this oil in the shower will give your skin maximum hydration. Last but not least, matcha powder protects the skin with antioxidants. Thanks to these antioxidants, minerals, and the magic of water, you will have soft and hydrated skin.

- 1 OZ (**30** G) MAGNESIUM SALT (OR COARSE SALT)
- 7 TBSP (**10** CL) VIRGIN COCONUT OIL
- 1 TSP MATCHA POWDER

WITCH'S SECRET

Use this scrub for your body, but not your face. Coconut oil is often fractionated, and because your face is more sensitive than the rest of your body, it may clog the pores. I suggest using jojoba oil if you wish to make this potion as a facial scrub because it is gentler but will do the job just as well.

⊛ Mix all the ingredients and put them in a closed jar.

⊛ Keep it in your bathroom and use it as an exfoliant every day.

Cacao-Coffee
DE CACAO·CAFÉ

  MAKES 1–2 MASKS 5 MINUTES

I'm a big believer in the magic of chocolate. In fact, I think you should even put it on your face. Cacao is rich in antioxidants that protect your skin from free radicals like pollution and UV rays, and coffee behaves in a similar way. These two beans purify the skin and will give you a healthy glow. You can even put this mask all over your body and use as a gentle exfoliant or as a strengthening hair mask. Ingredients that are good for our health and skin deserve to be at the center of our diet and beauty rituals.

- ⅓ OZ (**10** G) CACAO POWDER
- ⅓ OZ (**10** G) INSTANT COFFEE

✦ Combine the cacao powder and instant coffee in a small bowl and mix with a few drops of water until you have a paste that is neither too thin nor too thick.

✦ Apply the mask to your face and neck and leave on for 20 minutes before rinsing with warm water.

WITCH'S SECRET

To transform this mask into a scrub, massage your face with the cacao-coffee paste using small circular movements. You can also use coffee grounds for a scrub with a slightly rougher texture.

Mask
FOR TIRED EYES

  MAKES 1–2 MASKS 5 MINUTES

Bags under your eyes are often a sign of extreme fatigue. Witches know it's better to treat the cause of the problem instead of its symptoms, but they also know another way to get rid of dark circles. This under-eye beauty potion is made with the power of vitamin K found in watercress, spinach, and spirulina. Mixed with bentonite clay, which tightens the skin, and applied as a mask under the eyes, these ingredients promote blood circulation and diminish signs of fatigue. If you practice this beauty ritual regularly over a long period of time, it will prevent the appearance of dark circles altogether. When it comes to beauty and health, prevention is often more important than treatment.

- 1 KALE LEAF
- 1 HANDFUL OF WATERCRESS
- 1 HANDFUL OF SPINACH
- 2 TSP BENTONITE CLAY
- 2 TSP SPIRULINA

WITCH'S SECRET

Keep leftover paste in the freezer to avoid waste and to make sure you're always prepared to fight signs of fatigue. Defrost the potion in the refrigerator and just add a few drops of water before application because the cold might dry it out.

⊛ Remove the stem from the kale leaf and place all ingredients in a blender. Blend until smooth.

⊛ Apply the paste to your face and around your eyes in particular. Leave on for 20 minutes before rinsing with water.

Anti-Pollution
MASK

  MAKES 1-2 MASKS 5 MINUTES

We know how dangerous it is to have too much sun exposure, but we sometimes forget the damage pollution can do and the role it plays in contributing to premature skin aging. Luckily, there is a beauty potion whose immense powers can protect the skin. Blueberries, spinach, and spirulina are rich in protective antioxidants and help repair the skin, and parsley has one of the highest vitamin C levels of any plant based ingredient. In other words, to take full advantage of the magical powers of vegetables containing vitamin C, we should be eating them and applying them to our skin. Adding green clay to these ingredients purifies the skin and neutralizes pollution particles. To better protect yourself from the harmful effects of modern life, eat foods rich in antioxidants and put them *on* your body, too!

- **2** OZ **(50** G) BLUEBERRIES
- **1** HANDFUL OF FRESH SPINACH
- **½** BUNCH PARSLEY
- **1** TSP SPIRULINA
- **1** TSP GREEN CLAY

◉ Blend all of the ingredients in a blender.

◉ Apply the paste to your face regularly. Don't forget your neck—it needs protection, too.

WITCH'S SECRET

This mask is a perfect way to limit food waste. When your spinach and blueberries start looking a little worse for wear, just transform them into an anti-pollution mask.

Sun

OIL

  MAKES 1–2 JARS  3 HOURS + (INFUSION)

In this beauty spell, we invoke the magic of the sun to brighten the skin. The long winter months make the skin pale, and we need a healthy, suntanned look more than ever. The oils in this potion are rich in antioxidants to repair and stimulate tired skin. The omega-3 fatty acids nourish the skin better than any cream and the natural orange color of the carrot oil will give you a sun-kissed glow. And what's a sun magic spell without a little gold dust?

- 3½ TBSP **(5 CL)** CARROT OIL **(P. 179)**
- ⅛ TSP EDIBLE GOLD DUST
- 3½ TBSP **(5 CL)** JOJOBA OIL
- ¾ FLUID OZ **(2.5 CL)** ORGANIC SWEET ALMOND OIL

⊗ To prepare the carrot oil, refer to the recipe for Natural Sunscreen (p. 179).

⊗ Mix the gold dust with the carrot, jojoba, and sweet almond oils.

⊗ Apply a few drops of oil to your face in the morning to protect, nourish, and brighten your skin, especially when the weather is grey!

WITCH'S SECRET

You can also apply a few drops of this oil to your hair in summertime to protect it from the sun's rays. The gold dust will give your hair a magical shine.

- **Chase away bad vibes...** Sometimes you might feel like negative energies are attaching themselves to you. People will tell you it's all "in your head," but witches know the power of plants and have a spell to make these energies disappear. To remove negative energy, bacteria, or viruses from a room in your home, just burn a little bit of dried sage, a plant rich in neutralizing and antibacterial powers. Add a few dried sprigs of lavender or rosemary for more magic and to give the room a pleasant smell.

- **Understand the science behind sage magic ...** Magic and science are more closely related than we think: both of them have their foundation in nature. If we look at the world of particles, everything is defined by its "energetic charge." This charge is determined by the movement of energy. Lightning, rain, and seawater (because of the iodine it contains) are charged with negative ions. Stress, inflammation, and pain are charged with positive ions. When someone is going through a difficult time, a chemical reaction takes place that expels positive ions from the body. This is why a room vibrating with positive ions can be cleansed with the negative ions in neutralizing sage.

- **Practice mindfulness ...** Pay attention to yourself and to the rhythms and cycles of your body. We have lost many of our sensory and intuitive powers, but they are not forgotten forever. Follow your intuition.

- **Take a mineral bath ...** with a few spoonsful of Dead Sea salt, magnesium salt, or Epsom salt. For an evening bath, add dried lavender flowers. Don't have a bathtub? Take a footbath! The salt will help draw toxins from your body and release them through your feet.

- **Take curative showers ...** Tie eucalyptus leaves to your showerhead. The hot vapor will activate the plant's oils and help fight inflammation, headaches, stress, and muscle pain.

- **Spend time in nature ...** Take a walk in the forest, in a park, or anywhere with greenery. Go to the ocean as much as possible and go for a swim! Even in winter. Cold water reinvigorates the body!

- **Give yourself detox massages ...** During your shower, massage your entire body, starting with your feet and moving all the way up to your head. This little ritual improves blood circulation and helps purify the body and lymphatic system.

- **Take time for yourself ...** and your body first thing in the morning before starting your day. Do 10 minutes of yoga, stretching, or meditation.

- **Nighttime beauty rituals ...** When you take care of your body and give yourself the time to apply a face mask, put on cream before bed, or take a bath with essential oils, you are also taking care of your mental health and doing something kind for yourself.

- **Take advantage of the negative ions in the rain, wind, and sun ...** Practice yoga or meditation while nature is letting loose to help release stress and recharge with the energy of nature.

- **Fill your house with plant magic ...** Plants not only produce oxygen and remove toxins from the

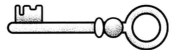

air, they also calm us and increase the release of endorphins.

- **Accept the passage of time...** Beauty never disappears, it evolves. And beauty that evolves leads to wisdom and power. This attitude will rejuvenate you.

- **Use crystals...** to feel more at peace, to dream, or to ease your pain. Their various structures can raise your energy level, neutralize negative thoughts, and help get rid of physical pain like headaches.

- **Live sustainably...** One of the most important values in witchcraft is protecting the earth. Reduce your waste, especially food waste, use natural and reusable products, and recycle when necessary.

- **Eat local . . .** Eat produce that comes from organic farms and stores. The farmers who grow these foods take care of the land and deserve our support. Local distribution means a lower carbon footprint and produce that can ripen in the earth and not during transportation.

- **Drink water infused with crystal magic...** Put quartz in a glass of water overnight to charge the liquid with healing properties. If you have shungite crystal, that's even better: This charged mineral will neutralize bacteria and toxins from the water.

- **Use less plastic...** When you can, make your own toothpaste, creams, soaps, and cleaning products. It's better for your health and for the planet.

- **Make your healing potions in advance...** Certain potions like tinctures need time to infuse.

To make sure you're always ready for any situation (illness, stress, etc.), prepare immunity potions and infusions ahead of time. As Shakespeare says in *Hamlet*, "The readiness is all". He was probably a bit of a witch himself.

- **Follow the cycles of the moon...** The new moon marks the beginning of a new cycle. This is a time of planning and positivity. The ascending moon marks a period of development, creativity, and transformation. The full moon is optimal for the practice of magic to achieve our goals. The descending moon is a time for relief and reflection.

WITCH'S SECRET

You don't need to scour forests and fields to harvest magical ingredients to fill your magic toolbox. All of these products can be found in organic grocery stores, herb shops, pharmacies, farmers' markets, and if all else fails, on the Internet.

y Culinary
SECRETS

• In nature, there is a balance between earth, water, fire, and air. And in recipes, we are always looking for a balance between fat, sugar, salt, and acidity. **Play around with these four elements to create new flavors.**

• **Cook vegetables the same way you would cook meat.** Marinated, cooked in wine, cooked in fat. . .

• Don't forget about aromatic herbs. . . they're good for more than just giving flavor. They reinforce the healing powers of food and can have magical effects even in small quantities. **Eating aromatic herbs in winter can help ensure stable health during this time of year.**

• **Do you have leftover stale bread? Don't throw it out!** Leave it in a sealed container overnight with a stalk of celery or a few lettuce leaves. It will absorb the humidity from these vegetables and be fresh again by morning.

• **To peel garlic with less hassle,** microwave the cloves for 15 seconds and the skins will come off by themselves.

• **Has your honey crystallized?** Leave it in the sun for a few hours and it will return to its original consistency.

• **Trying to spread cold butter on a slice of bread?** Just grate it! The little flakes of butter will melt more quickly and evenly.

• **To remove pesticides from fruits and vegetables,** soak them in a bath of water, a splash of white vinegar, and a few drops of lemon essential oil.

• **Did you buy aromatic herbs that are now starting to go bad?** Dry them for 30 seconds in the microwave on a sheet of parchment paper for later use. If you prefer fresh herbs, fill an ice cube tray with the herbs and some olive oil and freeze the mixture for future culinary spells.

• **Do you want your salmon or steak to be perfectly cooked?** Preheat the pan over high heat, sear the salmon or meat for a few minutes, then lower the heat. This will seal in the juices. This also works for mushrooms!

• **Are you tired of crying every time you peel onions?** Light a candle next to your cutting board and the irritating onion vapors will disappear.

• Drizzle a little olive oil over your cooked vegetables, meat, and fish right before serving. **Guaranteed shine!**

• **Let meat rest away from heat before serving.** For a whole chicken or roast, rest for 20 minutes, and 10 minutes for smaller cuts. Cover the meat with aluminum foil and a dish towel to keep it warm while the juices are pulled back in.

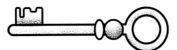

- **Save and freeze your (organic!) vegetable peelings.** Once you have enough, use them to make a broth. You can drink it by itself or use it to make soups, sautéed vegetables, and risottos.

- **If you overcrowd your pan,** your meat and vegetables may not sear properly because of the excess moisture. Opt for a larger size pan whenever possible.

- Add 1 little tsp of baking soda to the water when boiling eggs **to make it easier to remove the shell.**

- **Place a dish towel or paper towel in the bottom of your refrigerator** before putting away fruits and vegetables. It will absorb humidity that could damage them and contribute to rot.

- Put 1 or 2 bay leaves in your flour and rice jars **to protect them from insects.**

- **You put too much salt in your dish. All is not lost!** Add a raw potato to the dish and cook it for 10 minutes. The potato will absorb the excess salt. Save the potato in the freezer—it will be useful for making soups in the future.

- **Treat herbs like flowers.** Cut off the base of each stem and place the herbs in a glass in the refrigerator to keep them fresh longer.

Now it's your turn to meditate on everything I've shared with you.
Delight your loved ones and take care of your own health as well as theirs.

From now on, we are connected by magic...

Magic that you can now share with others—just I have shared with you—and which has been passed down from witches that came before us . . .

Recipe Index

For Ulysse

Thank you to Muriel for finding the witch in me.
To Frédérique for transforming my dream into a reality.

To Didier for believing in me and in this book.
To Diane, Christine, and Gwénola, and to everyone who collaborated on this culinary spellbook.

Thank you to Bob Bernstein, who encouraged me to write this cookbook and has supported me so much.

Thank you to Professor Claude Hamonet.

To all my doctors . . . and to my "alternative doctors."

Thank you to all the farmers, fishmongers, butchers, herbalists, and food artisans who provided all of these healing foods.

Thank you to Biocoop, Naturalia, Bio c' Bon, Monoprix, Casino, E.Leclerc, and La Grande Épicerie de Paris for providing magnificent ingredients for this book and for offering so many organic and eco-friendly products.

Thank you to my friends at Café Le Select and Café de Flore for hosting me during the writing of this book and for supplying me with hot chocolates.

Thank you to the emergency room doctors at Hôpital Cochin for operating on me after my knife faux pas.

And to my family, Greg, Lies, Daniel, and Carina, for supporting me so much on this voyage of health and life.

But above all, to Ulysse, who has been with me for every moment of this book's creation. He brings so much magic to my life.

☆

(And also to all the witches who make the world a little more magical)

Find Lisanna Wallance at www.CulinaryWitch.com and on Instagram @culinary.witch

TEXT
Lisanna Wallance
in collaboration with Muriel Teodori

Photography and Food and Prop Styling
Lisanna Wallance

EDITORIAL DIRECTOR
Didier Férat

EDITING
Diane Monserat

PROOFREADING
Christine Cameau and Gwénola de Chantérac

GRAPHIC DESIGN AND LAYOUT
Le Bureau des Affaires Graphiques

ASSISTANT GRAPHIC DESIGNER
Chloé Hart

PHOTOENGRAVING
Chromostyle

MANUFACTURING
Laurence Duboscq

Published originally under the title "Mes secrets de sorcière"
© 2019 Editions Solar, an imprint of Edi8, Paris
English translation copyright © 2020 by Skyhorse Publishing, Inc.

Skyhorse Publishing books may be purchased in bulk at special discounts for sales promotion, corporate gifts, fund-raising, or educational purposes. Special editions can also be created to specifications. For details, contact the Special Sales Department, Skyhorse Publishing, 307 West 36th Street, 11th Floor, New York, NY 10018 or info@skyhorsepublishing.com.

Skyhorse® and Skyhorse Publishing® are registered trademarks of Skyhorse Publishing, Inc.®, a Delaware corporation.

Visit our website at www.skyhorsepublishing.com.

10 9 8 7 6 5 4 3 2 1

Library of Congress Cataloging-in-Publication Data is available on file.

Cover design by Kai Texel
Cover photos by Lisanna Wallance

Print ISBN: 978-1-5107-5943-5
Ebook ISBN: 978-1-5107-5981-7

Printed in China